More Advance Praise for *Real Teams Win*

Steding has proven repeatedly in his work as a CEO that he knows exactly what needs to be done to build and lead a *real* team. If you follow his process, you'll be able to create a team that will accomplish more, faster than ever before.

> Dr. Dan Thomas, PhD, CEO Focus, Inc.
> and author of *Business Sense*

Steding's work underscores the richness and power of creativity over a task-oriented approach. His book *Real Teams Win,* his guidance and his consulting skills are invaluable for all CEO's across industries. Now more than ever, Tom's wisdom will make transformational change possible.

> Michela Abrams, Founder MOCA+, former CEO Dwell Media

The myth of the omnipotent CEO makes great press but damages its leaders and employees. *Real Teams Win* describes a better way to build high performance organizations through creative collaboration, creating a blueprint of Enterprise, Culture, Mindset and the practices and principles necessary to implement a new culture—one that where both the people and company thrive and excel.

> Steve Blank, Defense Business Board at US DoD,
> and author of *The Startup Owner's Manual*

Tom Steding begins his book, *Real Teams Win,* by asserting that to understand how an organization really works, it is much more useful to look at its internal networks that show how information and influence really flow than to rely on a traditional org chart that indicate only formal relationships. He also argues that building strong teams is more critical to the success of a business than finding a heroic leader. Steding uses these insights as jumping-off points to describe in detail the principles and practices that organizations need to adopt in order to create a healthy culture and sustain productive teams. Steding's book is an artful blend of theory drawn from a variety of disciples including mythology and psychology, and practical advice that is firmly grounded in his extensive experience working with a wide range of companies.

Richard Adler, Distinguished Fellow, Institute for the Future

In this timely, remarkable, emotionally intelligent presentation of a truly twenty-first century vision of leadership, Dr. Steding offer an engaging, deceptively "easy" read of how his deep understanding of complexity can be transformatively applied to teams in organizations. Having put his principles into practice, I can attest to their efficacy. In a nutshell, creative collaboration engenders group wisdom which, when applied to the business sector, achieves far more than any individual, no matter the genius. *Real Teams Win* yields magic results.

Joseph Cambray, PhD, President/CEO,
Pacifica Graduate Institute

Since the start of the Industrial Age, businesses have been built on a mechanical model that in no way, shape or form maps to the most effective ways for humans to work together. Tom Steding has made the compelling case that collaborative teams built on the uniquely powerful human capacity for empathy are the ones that produce the most astounding results. But way beyond making the case for this, Tom has created the effective, practical, Blueprint for our time in his great book, *Real Teams Win*. I am thrilled that now business leaders at all levels will get to benefit from the Blueprint through this book.

Betsy Burroughs, President, FocusCatalyst
and author of FOCUS

Steding has been leading teams in Silicon Valley for 40 years, including more than a dozen startups. He has seen it all. His perspective on authentic, effective leadership is valuable to seasoned executives, aspiring leaders and first-time managers.

David Spreng, Founder, CEO & CIO at Runway Growth Capital

Building and growing a business is hard. Especially so since most entrepreneurs and managers start with a faulty view of leadership. Tom Steding's book, *Real Teams Win*, brings over 40 years of management experience to provide a practical Blueprint for building the high-performance teams needed for a successful business today. Steding's insight goes beyond acknowledging the importance of corporate culture. He provides the framework and steps to establish the mindset needed to create highly effective teams.

Reid Rutherford, Managing Partner, 1Flourish Capital

As a CEO seeking best leadership practice while running multiple companies, both public and private, *Real Teams Win* arrives as a breakthrough treatment of the topic. Tom Steding has reinforced what I always thought was an important part of my approach and takes it even further. I heartily recommend this for CEO reading, but also for anyone in the organization looking for a more meaningful and effective approach to their respective roles.

Doug Cole, CEO, American Battery Technology Company

Unlike most business books that try to turn a simple idea in to 250 pages, Tom Steding lifts the veil on the next generation of leadership philosophy that evolved in Silicon Valley over the past decade. Building upon psychology breakthroughs pioneered by Dr. Howard Teich, I saw Tom embody the true essence of leading with empathy. However, the insights go much deeper and create the foundation for an entirely new way to achieve high performance in organizations.

B. Ray Conley, CEO Benetic, former CEO
CreekStone Capital Management, LLC
and Managing Partner Golden Oak Ventures

Distilling hard-earned learnings from leading over a dozen tech startups, Tom Steding offers an elegantly simple but difficult-to-master framework for fostering the true teamwork absolutely essential to a high-performing organization. Eminently practical yet enjoyable to read, Tom draws upon the lessons taught by mythology over the centuries to illustrate how each of us can leverage our unique attributes to be more effective in working within environments characterized better by amorphous networks than by defined organizational charts.

Richard Stuebi, President/Founder of Future Energy Advisors, Senior Fellow at Boston University Institute for Sustainable Energy, former consultant at McKinsey & Co.

In a world awash in chaos, *Real Teams Win* provides a beacon of clarity to guide leaders across all sectors of organizational form to transcend the din of disorienting events that exist today where networks trump hierarchies and people compete to cooperate. Steding has produced an indispensable guide to anyone tasked with transforming their organization for the next generation of human challenges.

William Steding, PhD, author of *Saving America in the Age of Deceit*

I have known and worked with Tom Steding in senior management roles for over 20 years, and I have had the good fortune to observe firsthand his Blueprint in action. Tom has not only written *Real Teams Win*, he has lived it. His ability to bring together disparate groups of people to create highly effect teams who "get things done" is unmatched. Everyone, from team members to CEOs, needs to read this book.

Linda Hayes, CEO, Linda Hayes Consulting, former CEO, Andale, Inc.

REAL TEAMS WIN

*What Smart Leaders
Need to Know Now About
Achieving Peak Performance*

THOMAS L. STEDING, PH.D.

Humanix Books

www.humanixbooks.com

Humanix Books
Real Teams Win

Humanix Books, P.O. Box 20989, West Palm Beach, FL 33416, USA
www.humanixbooks.com | info@humanixbooks.com

Humanix Books is a division of Humanix Publishing, LLC. Its trademark,
consisting of the words "Humanix Books," is registered in the Patent and
Trademark Office and in other countries.

ISBN: 978-1-630-06157-9 (Hardcover)
ISBN: 978-1-630-06158-6 (E-book)

Printed in the United States of America
10 9 8 7 6 5 4 3 2 1

Dedicated to family, the best of life:

Carole, Anna, Doug, Ateev, LeeAnn, Ria, Joby,

Naveen, SamTom, Carolyne, Sugar, Biscuit,

Leo, Ursa, Ara, Max, Ozzie, and Indy,

all resulting from an original blind date

on a Friday the Thirteenth

AUTHOR'S NOTE

I n a book declaring war on narcissism, I am particularly reluctant to use the pronoun "I" (including in this sentence). So "I" is only used where the topic is solely associated with myself. Otherwise, "we" will refer first to collaboration with my inspired partner, Dr. Howard Teich, and also to all the wonderful colleagues mentioned in the Acknowledgments who have supported the development of this material.

CONTENTS

Preface
Why This Book? xi

CHAPTER 1
Leadership Involves People 1

CHAPTER 2
Real versus Fake Teams 5

PART I

Changing Leadership and the New Model

CHAPTER 3
Mandate for Change
The Hierarchical Leadership Model Is Increasingly Obsolete 13

CHAPTER 4
Intimations of a New Leadership Model
Creative Collaboration Is Profitable 19

CHAPTER 5
The New Model of Leadership
A Network, Not a Hierarchy 25

CHAPTER 6

Blueprint: Delivering the New Model

Leadership Journey from Innovation to Execution   31

INTERLUDE: Myth and the Hero's Journey   35

PART II

Diagnostic System
The What of Leadership

CHAPTER 7

The Hidden to Be Revealed

That Which Is Not Acknowledged Rules *Outcome*   45

CHAPTER 8

Mindset Malware

Leadership Dysfunction Is Common and Often Unrecognized   57

CHAPTER 9

Dimensions of Culture and Enterprise

Understanding the Culture and Enterprise Layers   61

PART III

Foundation Principles
The Why of Leadership

CHAPTER 10

Setting It Up

What Teams Want   69

INTERLUDE: The Mythological Basis of Complementarity   71

CHAPTER 11

Principles—Complementarity

A Basic Rule of Nature 77

CHAPTER 12

Complementarity in Leadership 85

CHAPTER 13

Going Deeper

Complementary Archetypes: Solar/Lunar 91

INTERLUDE: From Solo Hero to Complementary Heroes 95

CHAPTER 14

More Going Deeper

Complementary Archetypes: Puer/Senex 103

INTERLUDE: Daedalus and Icarus/Helios and Phaeton 107

CHAPTER 15

Principles—Empathy

The Master Emotion 111

CHAPTER 16

Beyond Emotional Intelligence

Emotional Integrity 119

CHAPTER 17

Collaboration: How to Do Empathy

Empathy/Challenge 123

CHAPTER 18

Marketing and Empathy

Real Marketing 129

CHAPTER 19

Nonattachment

Enabling Creative Dialogue   139

INTERLUDE: The Myth of Narcissus   143

CHAPTER 20

Lessons from Narcissus

Dangers of Self-Centeredness in the Team   147

CHAPTER 21

The Paradox of Success and Failure

A Redemptive Narrative   153

CHAPTER 22

Idealized Expectations: Cancer of the Mind

Roadblock to a Creative Culture   157

PART IV

Practices

The How of Leadership

CHAPTER 23

Communication Practice

The Role of Communication in Team Performance   169

CHAPTER 24

Case Study: NASA

Catastrophic Consequences of Poor Communication   179

INTERLUDE: Cultivating Wisdom with Myth   183

CHAPTER 25
Commitment Practice
Real versus False Commitments   187

CHAPTER 26
Closure Practice
A Neglected Practice   193

CHAPTER 27
Cultural Fabric
How Principles Support Effective Cultural Practices   201

CHAPTER 28
Toward Cultural Transformation
A Sealed Container Eliminates Leakage and Loss   203

CHAPTER 29
The Self-Regulating Organization
Evolution and Radiation   207

INTERLUDE: Drama and Dionysus   213

CHAPTER 30
Process
The Full Life-Cycle Journey from Innovation to Execution   219

INTERLUDE: Feminine Myths   223

INTERLUDE: The Myths That Mystify   229

PART V

Blueprint in Action
Implementing Blueprint

CHAPTER 31

Blueprint in Action
An Integrated Framework for High Performance   235

CHAPTER 32

Implementing Blueprint: Dealing with Resistance
The Challenge   243

CHAPTER 33

Implementing Blueprint: Realizing the Benefits
The Reward   245

Further Reading   249

Acknowledgments   253

Index   257

PREFACE

Why This Book?

t seems I've been trying to answer questions about leadership my entire career. This sometimes-quixotic quest seems to be rooted in an obsession to improve the system around me. Inside, I felt a deep impulse to fix things, maybe out of guilt for damn near burning down the house next door at age five by setting its trash container on fire. Or maybe it was the fire itself that was the important element: to fire things up, to light a fire under the system, to have fire in the belly, and sometimes simply to misfire. Nonetheless, over time I became obsessed with the "possibility" of things, and the sense that with a little more effort—and awareness—matters could be substantially better.

With over four decades in the high-tech industry, this search often felt like random groping toward an ideal of truly effective leadership, sometimes breaking into the light, but other times simply bumping into walls. It involved a succession of decade-long intervals (being a slow learner) through multiple layers of method, in a search for that leadership effectiveness. Each layer revealed its limitations and took me to a deeper level, culminating in the method described here in *Real Teams Win*, the *Blueprint* framework presented in this book: a journey in depth. I felt I should describe that journey, to hopefully save you time in your own search.

More than half of that career has been involved in running start-ups, those fast-cycle laboratories of creativity and enthusiasm. Indeed, my startup interest became my own obsessive-compulsive disorder, with no known cure, and given that at the time of this writing I am on startup number 13, the 12-step recovery program apparently didn't work out for me either. Nevertheless, the challenges of dealing with new environments, new teams, and new challenges every two years or so provided rich material for an evolving leadership approach. And somehow I have avoided ever having to turn out the lights.

So, let's take a look as we enter this drama in medias res.

OPTIMAL CONTROL

At the beginning of my journey, I found myself with a bunch of other smartass Ph.D.'s also fresh out of school trying to apply electrical engineering's Optimal Control Theory ("finding a control law for a given system such that a certain optimality criterion is achieved") to anything that moved. Our preferred targets were big hairy complex systems like multistate electric grids that tended to shut down when a tree branch fell on a power line, and a huge ballistic missile defense system set up to keep an attack of 300 Soviet ICBM missiles from raining down on our Minuteman missile fields in North Dakota. Good luck with that. One of the challenges was that the incoming booster tank of an ICBM, upon reentering the atmosphere, would break into 300 or so pieces, each with a radar cross-section similar to that of a nuclear warhead. My problem was to figure out which one was the warhead. This was called the Bulk Filter. It should have been called Run Like Hell.

While the company made interesting contributions in many applications, including even creating some new industries, we certainly didn't become Masters of the Universe (which seemed to me the unspoken intent).

STRATEGY

Eventually, having fulfilled Hayakawa's assertion that it takes 10 years to get over the effect of a Ph.D., I discovered the Stanford Sloan program, a 10-month mid-career program for executives, that is part of its Graduate School of Business. I oh-so-selflessly volunteered to participate on my company's behalf, and to my utter astonishment, gained its approval. What followed was, for me, something akin to a religious conversion, replete with its own icons, such as the Capital Asset Pricing Model and the Principal–Agent Theory. It was there I discovered the magic elixir for fixing things: strategy. Here was my new path to becoming Master of the Universe.

When I returned from the program, British Petroleum had bought my company and we were now part of a business stream comprising seven companies and 3,000 professionals. My sandbox thus increased tenfold. With the help of gifted advisers, I took on developing a strategic management process and considered myself one of the leading strategic thinkers in our group. I now knew exactly how to fix things. Yeah, right.

Well, it did kind of work. Strategic skills are an important part of creating quality organizations, but there seemed to be this annoying problem that people didn't just go do what was specified. Strategy passed the necessity test (without it, you probably fail), but flunked the sufficiency test (with it, you could *not* fail). Humans were the problem, and unfortunately there didn't seem a way to build a company without them.

OPERATIONAL MANAGEMENT

I was then given overall operational management responsibility for a company with the annoying requirement that we actually get things done. I designed brilliant organizational schemes and innovative systems, only to have a fresh on-the-ground encounter with inertia. Something else had to be done. So, I got interested in processes and practices to restrain the errant workings of those intractable people on the team. I hired the future co-author of my first book to deliver teamwork training. Now I knew I was onto something useful. I recall, for example, being blown away by the distinction between an authentic and false commitment, how the latter is made automatically and how it degrades performance (all to be covered later in this book). I hired an outstanding coach who understood the Hermetic principle of communication, also described later. I also hired a leading project management expert to train the team on how to keep projects on track, ensure compliance, and avoid underbidding on large contracts by 50% like the company had done before. Now I really knew how to fix things.

Again, it kind of worked. Sure, we got some benefit from it, but I was left with nagging doubts about the whole approach. Basically, the method was rational: If you do this, if you follow these practices, it will work. But then, why didn't people follow the practices? What else was at work?

BUILT ON TRUST

By now, I had moved on to running startups. My first involved a high-profile email encryption company whose themes—privacy, encryption, security—still resonate today. In fact, we put the issue of "privacy" on the map, with a company described by some in the press as "The marketing gorilla of the Internet." Somehow, intuitively, I based the culture of the company on explicit operating principles—a values-based approach. The result was an extremely enthusiastic and energized team, and great appreciation across the majority of the team for a memorable and meaningful work experience. However, other factors (at the time hidden) interceded and caused the company to fail to realize its full potential. This early experience raised the essential question "What the hell just happened?" What followed was the hunt for how to build on the brilliant part, while avoiding falling prey to dysfunctional behavior. It also inspired publication of a book titled *Built on Trust: How to Gain Advantage in Any Organization* that explained how earned trust can create competitive advantage.

MINDSET

I was introduced by a colleague to Dr. Howard Teich, a San Francisco psychotherapist and coach. Howard had a compelling track record in transforming leadership in a number of organizations. His focus was on radical use of empathy and eradicating idealized expectations ("cancer of the mind"). Here I found something fresh, a new path for leadership, and we instantly hit it off. Together, we developed key concepts defining a new layer in the organizational ecosystem: *Mindset*. Our focus was on the hidden, or unacknowledged, factors that influence outcome, and that even *rule* them. Mindset opened up a new domain for understanding the root causes for outcome. We then saw how to *engineer* culture, which suggested extending the oft-repeated assertion that "culture eats strategy for lunch" and rewrote it to argue that "mindset eats culture for breakfast." Also, counterintuitively, we showed how the method can increase performance while frequently *decreasing* expenses. Our collaboration led us to the answer of what really motivates people, and also revealed to us why intellectual prescriptions for leadership often simply don't work.

Then something really weird happened: I developed empathy. This was not just from pursuing the concept out of intellectual curiosity, rather, it was a result of Howard's insistence in mercilessly pounding the practice of empathy into my head. Paradoxically, instead of generating anxiety about entering into the emotional world of people and the team, it offered a new and liberating sense of objectification: seeing more clearly the reality of the local emotional state, which was the bedrock for determining direction and outcome. Rather than imposing my will of an alleged superior approach to fixing things, I was liberated from my narcissistic opinions of how things should be, and instead saw the underlying emotional currents as they really were and how to work with them without prejudice. I had descended from my lofty perch of mathematical optimizer, master strategist, and operational drill sergeant. I had gone completely native.

Our work together led to characterizing those deeper layers in the system and to defining principles enabling improved (let's not say "optimal") performance. Now I could understand how the public company CEO, who bragged incessantly about his great culture, received an employee survey that said the majority of employees hated it. And how the VP of Sales could not get out of her self-centeredness and really hear the CEO, causing her to subsequently lose her job. And also why one could predict that an arrogant CTO, who would not permit his team to fix his product design, eventually caused it to burst into flames on a customer's premise. These and many other answers will be covered in this book.

This book is geared to leaders. In one segment, that includes top management: CEOs, COOs, EVPs, and Chairmen or Chairwomen. However, it also targets mid-management leaders who want to increase the performance of their teams. Further, it targets individuals, those inspired folks who understand their own opportunity to "lead from their position," offering creative suggestions, the diagnosis of problems, and how to cover the backs of their buddies.

A warning. ... This book doesn't promise riches, but it does offer a better way to organize teams and to encourage, recognize, and make the most of serendipitous positive outcomes—positive in terms of finances, performance, and values. Chance favors the prepared culture.

Becoming a part of the emotional life of a team may engender discomfort for some. So, if psychological dialogue makes you feel all squirmy, and terms like "emotion" and "psyche" send shivers up your spine, and if you think effective leadership is all about intellect and charisma and technology, this approach may not be for you. If you believe a well-crafted strategy is sufficient for success, if you use the tell-and-sell approach as your method of inspiration, if you are an ardent practitioner of constructive confrontation (emphasis on confrontation), and cannot fathom a reason to change, you'll find I'm writing in a different language. If so, stop here and request a refund.

I aim to engender insight, not provoke discomfort—and I've had plenty of experience with both.

Finally, this book declares war on narcissism (while attempting to avoid my own narcissism in suggesting everyone else should reform). To me, too often the high-tech world is caught in its own inflation, which resides like mildew in the dark corners of our workspaces. We are often deservedly proud of our extraordinary contributions toward a better world, while ignoring their occasional downsides. We would benefit by keeping in mind Robinson Jeffers' admonition about man's "stupid dreams and red rooster importance: Let him count the star-swirls."

CHAPTER 1

LEADERSHIP
INVOLVES PEOPLE

In order to lead, you need to understand what motivates people.
When you motivate people, you and your company win.
—TOM STEDING

D o you feel disengaged from your work? Do you experience your work life as devoid of meaning or inspiration? Do you often feel neither seen nor heard? Do you witness unchallenged trickery in your organization? Do you hear rampant gossip? Do you wonder how management can make such boneheaded decisions and yet feel unable to challenge them? Or as a leader do you sometimes feel you are talking to a brick wall?

Much of the current leadership narrative that focuses on top-down, machine-based orientation does not take into account the human drama played out in the office, where the heart beats and longs for more than a nine-to-five act of economic necessity. However, in order for business to survive, thrive, and remain competitive as it moves into the future, an entirely new concept of the organization is required.

This book offers a comprehensive framework and toolkit to bring creativity, insight, and meaning to the workplace. *Real Teams Win* establishes a new arena where the human spirit can flourish, accessing the superior intelligence of the connected team. Using proven principles, practices, structure, and processes, *Real Teams Win* provides new pathways to inventive ideas, newly designed products, and unique visions. It also has a self-renewing effect, a sustaining capacity for continuous reinvention, and is a generator of businesses that are more than just a one-time play. It builds on the basic realization that creativity is an emergent property of a system properly configured.

When we envision the organization as a living organism with a vibrant inner life and realize that the task of leadership is to encourage its evolution at the highest level, we enter a new frontier in the search for competitive advantage.

The *Blueprint* framework in this book emerged from a recognition that the underlying principles and practices for both innovation and execution phases in development—whether a project or product or company—are the same. Within this field of shared meaning, imagine being part of a high-performance team with a distinct competitive advantage, or improving a high potential but underperforming team, or creating an effective team from the ground up. If you feel disengaged from your work, you can now find new engagement, and if you feel your work life is devoid of meaning, you can experience the magic of deep connection and purpose. If you feel your worklife is underperforming, you've come to the right place.

The *Blueprint* approach relies on a *depth perspective*. The factors that determine, even rule, outcome lie in the deeper layers of the organization and its people. Coming to terms with those factors is key to resolving problems and discovering creative new paths. There we encounter authentic human needs: to be seen and heard, to contribute and to be recognized for our contribution, and to engage in the transcendent urge to be part of something bigger than ourselves, something transcendent that reflects our core values. Something meaningful. Lasting.

Our starting point is often hiding in plain sight. It's the observation that virtually all persistent business problems have a psychological root. The key word here is "persistent." Business problems of one sort or another never cease. But *persistent* business problems are a different matter. Carl Jung famously said, "Neurosis is always a substitute for legitimate suffering." The same thought can be applied to teams. Unfortunately, instead of doing the hard and painful work to confront self-defeating habits within the teams or challenging external circumstances, leadership too often prefers to pretend such problems do not exist, or simply neglect to even consider their possibility.

We can assume that people are rational and that forces in play in business are explicit and visible. And that's true, to varying degrees. But hidden factors are nearly *always* in play and nearly *always* unarticulated. In our experience, it is a rare case in which there wasn't some unacknowledged causative factor driving events. This is the notion of the "root cause," that final stopping point of a diagnosis where you have the sense you have gotten to the bottom of the matter and need look no further.

If all of this sounds too philosophical for your tastes, be assured that the methods we describe are firmly grounded and well tested in various settings, starting with the principles and practices described here in *Real Teams Win*. Throughout this book, you will read stories of success and stories of failure. Some long, some short, some ongoing. These are all real companies (though some have been disguised to protect the innocent, and also the not-so-innocent but well-intentioned). A few examples provide a sneak peek at the power of the implementation framework we've developed and established over the years and have set forth here:

- An enterprise software company with $32M invested over seven years with little traction. Once we adopted the leadership approach described in this book, results appeared quickly. Within six months, we more than doubled bookings over the prior year, *reduced cash burn from $2M per quarter to $54K* per quarter, successfully implemented a new strategy, and acquired premier customers.

- A message assurance company with over $20M invested over five years with no growth. Within 12 months, we had grown new business 87% quarter-to-quarter over four quarters, won multiple industry awards, including Technology of the Year from InfoWorld, acquired more than 500 new customers, and increased the average selling price 50 times. All while *reducing headcount and expenses 25%*.

- An optoelectronics company that had used $65M of R&D over 25 years with no product and no commercial capability. Using this system, within 18 months we had overhauled the company and recruited a new management team, *cut burn rate in half*, developed commercially compelling foundry services, produced two prototypes ahead of schedule, acquired a lead customer, and exceeded the prior management's quarterly revenue by over 300%.

One of the most striking aspects of these three pilots is that we were able to dramatically improve performance *while cutting expenses*, as noted earlier. This casts doubt on the assumption that outcome requires expenditure. It doesn't. It requires leadership.

CHAPTER 2

REAL VERSUS FAKE TEAMS

Real teams win. By "real," we mean a living system built around creative collaboration, intuition, and trust, that dramatically downplays the role of ego, power-tripping, and the will to dominate. We call for a new mandate for leadership: to develop and nurture an environment that is collaborative, creative, agile, supple, non-oppositional, and courageous. This vision for real teams opens vast new territory for exploration and development—both within the organization and within each of us as individuals. There is much we can learn through the principles and practices in this book, from each other, across generations, and from the ages.

Real teams don't worry about whether the boss is in a good mood today or not. Real teams loathe politics. Real teams spend their emotional energy focusing on the mission and figuring out how they can contribute. Real teams think gossip is for people who are taking their eye off the ball and not contributing to positive success. Real teams care as much about their colleagues as themselves. Real teams don't look over their shoulders. Real teams don't carry resentments but off-load and resolve them as conflicts arise. Real teams see commitments as an opportunity to shine, not as obligations to evade.

The alternative to a real team is a pretend or fake team. Almost everyone has experienced this at one time or another. People who publicly talk about the value of teamwork but who actually hate each other. People who gossip about their peers, the company, and management, but who never come up with any solutions to actually solve problems. Situations where sudden slippage appears out of nowhere. Meetings are endless with no resolution. Conversations are confrontational and offputting, ending with the fruitless "agree to disagree." Leaders don't listen, and team members stop contributing after the last smackdown they got in yesterday's meeting. Morale is bad, and performance is deteriorating.

Real teams win in two ways: one internal; the other external. Externally, benefits include the performance of the entity measured in the usual metrics of growth, profitability, and brand success. Internally, they involve generating a meaningful work life for the participants. Now the team has the uncommon experience of creative collaboration without persistent toxicity, realizes the transcendent joy of a healthy connection with a bigger mission beyond personal ego boundaries, and celebrates how this team manifests its unique creativity in external performance factors via the applause that follows a brilliant performance. The *Blueprint* framework offers both by joining a deeper understanding of the underlying root causes for execution with the principles, practices, and processes for execution.

NARCISSISM AND SURRENDER OF THE EGO

The key factor underlying team dysfunctionality is narcissism or self-centeredness, either across the team or especially in its leadership. The *Blueprint* approach is predicated on the mandate that *all* members of the organization—bottom to top—must surrender their ego in order to create an organization that functions at top capacity. The ego mind is, of course, essential to who we are. Clearly, we could not have evolved to our current state, with all of mankind's achievements, without the ego. Yet the ego mind also includes its own bizarre combination of biases, misperceptions, defenses, strange beliefs, selfish longings, and irrational fears. And it is this part of the ego that inhibits true creativity. To establish a high-performance team, real teams require egos subdued to a common purpose. In order to overcome any one particular ego malfunction in any individual team member, the organization must access the collective intelligence of the team. By "surrendering" their ego, we mean the process by which individuals defer to the overall superior intelligence of the connected team, which typically does not share our own peculiar eccentricities that often block our creative path.

We know that companies with dysfunctional leadership (a.k.a., "screwed up") can be successful, at least for a while. More often than not, however, if you are screwed up, you're probably going to screw up. Many of these cases involve excessive ego, and where ego soars, souls suffer. Yet even these companies can be successful with new technology and fortuitous timing. We've seen it happen. We've also seen tyrannical leadership carry on for an impressive period of time. In addition, we know from experience that companies can do better with the method we describe. And *better* is the goal.

MYTH AND LEADERSHIP

At the U.S. Army Armor School, a story is told (perhaps apocryphal) that the first tank assault in WWI was so successful it drove forward into enemy lines 30 miles ... and ran out of gas. Similarly, in today's world we are at risk of outrunning our supply line of hard-earned wisdom within the constraints of human nature. In search of a remedy, we look to myths that have provided guidance through the ages—relevant wisdom that we are at risk of losing.

So, what do myths have to do with leadership? Turns out, a lot. Leadership is about people. And the more you know about people, the more effective leadership can be to achieve desired results. A possibly underutilized resource to understand people is this mythic layer, the deeper region of our psyche that is expressed in the themes and drama of our ancient stories.

In order to understand their importance, take a look at how myths came to be. In the Greek pantheon, for example, figures and stories were made up based on projections (attributing your own feelings and attitudes onto another person or object, often unconsciously) of various aspects of the human psyche. So, our warrior instincts were located in the invented figure Ares, feminine qualities in Aphrodite, and strength and power in Hercules. Mirroring the complexity of humans, they necessarily appeared in droves. As such, they are a readout of our own humanity, the operating system of us as people—and if you want to understand how an operating system works, read the source code. Along the way, we examine multiple stories from mythological traditions to illuminate the aspects of humanity relevant to effective leadership. We will invite heroes and heroines from ancient mythology into the room, only to discover they have been there all along.

One of the problems may be that myths suffer from the idea that myths are, well, myths, and therefore aren't true. This misses the point that, while myths may be factually untrue, they contain important truths that we can learn from.

We also suggest linkages that may offer insight into leadership and the human experience in teams. We understand that myths and their underlying archetypes—the original pattern or model from which all things of the same kind are copied or on which they are based—have limitless paths and implications. Our intent is to suggest a bridge connecting the world of myths to the world of organizational teamwork, and allow the ensuing foot traffic to proceed as it will.

To access the wisdom of myths for leadership, it is necessary to toggle back and forth between the depth of ancient myth and the surface of modern business practice, endeavoring to merge these two into an integrated and expanded consciousness. This toggle effect does require keeping the old and new in mind simultaneously. Be patient and give it a try. You will find yourself increasingly able to move between two domains of thought. Don't worry, you don't need to study mythology, just to reflect on the significance of the exemplary tales interspersed throughout *Real Teams Win.*

Understanding mythic patterns in our contemporary workplace exposes previously unacknowledged forces, alerts us to new creative paths, and provides confidence that our leadership is in tune with authentic human qualities. Understanding and respecting the power of archetypes provides a more solid grounding for leadership than following some patchwork intellectual method conceived by the ego mind anxious to conceal its befuddlement about things that go awry in unexpected directions for unexplained reasons.

For example, as we learn to detect narcissism in the team, we then recall that one of the problems Narcissus exhibited was a failure to take input, and we are alerted to the fact that somewhere our team may be missing the boat. When we call for heroic action, we also recall that Hercules in all his admirable strength was also a bit of a dodo, shooting arrows at the sun to lower the temperature and impetuously running off in disastrous directions. We understand that he anticipated today's increasing failure of the Solo Hero Model, and we need to look for new directions for better results. We also then recall Athena with a much more balanced approach (courage/compassion, logic/creativity, mediator/warrior), who also rescued Hercules and provides today a model of complementarity in leadership, which we promote. We also recognize Hermes, the God of Complementarity, at work when we see tricksterism afoot—sometimes necessary and often painful—but we also recognize his critical contribution to opening paths of communication ("the Hermetic Method") enabling creative dialogue and systematic transformation.

One of the author's favorite mythic figures is Pan, the Greek god of wooded spaces and pastures. Now, one of the author's colleagues was heard to say, "There are a million ways for startups to go wrong," referring to a dismal gallery to which the author has made his own unique contributions. Pan's wild, erratic, and sometimes destructive nature seems to be the personification of how reality often proceeds.

Hillman tells us "Noon is Pan's hour," the moment of bright light where we pridefully celebrate our own genius as Master of Ceremonies getting to a great moment, only to have a terrifying encounter with chaos. It behooves the leader sensing clear skies and exciting growth to keep a watchful eye out for Pan creeping through the surrounding wilderness and heading to the campsite to carry out his mischief.

With the stage set, let's jump in and examine the mandate for the New Leadership Model.

PART I

Changing Leadership and the New Model

CHAPTER 3

MANDATE FOR CHANGE

The Hierarchical Leadership Model Is Increasingly Obsolete

The top-down, command-and-control, tell-and-sell, solo heroic, ego-based mindset is increasingly ineffective. It still persists though. We hear it in fixed opinions and dogmatic expressions. We see it when people refuse to hear another's point of view. We see it when they are openly dismissive and run over others' ideas like a flatiron. We see it when leaders remain oblivious to the effect of their management style on their team and deny any role in suboptimal performance. And we see it in the pervasive arrogance of power.

Underlying this approach is the long predominant, although mostly unconscious, *organization-as-machine* metaphor. Consider some of the management fads gone by: Taylor time studies; growth/share manufacturing efficiency; downsizing, upsizing, rightsizing; time-based competition. These view the organization from the outside as a mechanism to be adjusted and optimized. This metaphor insinuates the necessity of a superior control function steeped in the esoteric traditions of control, and leadership becomes the province of the technocratically adept pulling levers (or turning gears as the graphic suggests). Manager as puppeteer; people as marionettes. This approach is illustrated in Figure 3-1.

FIGURE 3-1 The Old Leadership Model

Hierarchical leadership is also often suppressive and plain wrong. I have seen cases where leadership made decisions that were clearly wrong but still forced them on the team, which led to hundreds of millions of dollars in losses. Imagine if, alternatively, the leadership had encouraged *trusting, open, realistic,* and *creative dialogue* instead of the top-down model. Given the obvious error of the path under consideration, somebody would raise a concern. Open, safe, and creative dialogue would follow. The leader, understanding his or her lack of monopoly on good ideas, might have agreed to a better path.

THE SILENT MAJORITY: GALLUP SAYS 69% OF U.S. WORKERS ARE EITHER "NOT ENGAGED" OR "ACTIVELY DISENGAGED"

Imagine what this looks like in your conference room. You are sitting in your team meeting when you suddenly realize that the person to your right, and the person to your left, are mostly just a 98.6° radiating body, playing its thermodynamic role as a warm spot in the room. This is beginning to look less like a team and more like a waiting room in a funeral parlor. Essentially lacking two-thirds of its potential talent, you see the team has taken a hit. Even worse, this causes a numbing effect on the remaining one-third of the room's personnel who are actually trying to get something done. Life among the detractors sucks the energy and enthusiasm out of the office atmosphere.

So, who are these people? Are they holding back and clutching desperately to their jobs simply out of survival anxiety? "Give me a job and I will sit here," they're thinking, "but don't ask anything of my soul or inner being, because that is where I really live, and it isn't for sale." Or are they still suffering from some early career trauma where they did speak up and tried to contribute and got nailed in the process? Fallout from the "never again" syndrome.

This reminds me of my own experience. I once joined a choir of 125 people, despite telling the choir director I couldn't sing. Well, it turned out that I could sing, but unfortunately I was an octave below the bass section. So, I was sent off to take additional opera singing lessons that lasted three years. During this time, I learned that most people think they can't sing because somebody told them early on that they couldn't. In my case, perhaps my antipathy toward the practice was due to this big guy punching my 140-pound weakling body during choir practice in high school. But now you know: You can sing, and you can contribute, and you can speak up. So, belt it out.

To this silent majority, I want more from you. I want to hear your "stupid" ideas, befriend them anyway (without rejection, judgment, or dismissal) to discover the gem lying disguised under their unpleasant cover. I want to see joy in your eyes when you realize you just surprised yourself with something really good and original. I want to know if you don't like what is going on and work with you on that, rather than have you smolder with resentment in silence, or worse, engage in malicious compliance, nodding yes and meaning no. I want more from you for you. I care for you, and I want you to care for you, too. I want to bask in the warmth of a vibrant aura around the team, enjoy the energy in the room, feel the heat. I want to see your sparkle, your firework display celebrating your liberated creativity and independence. I want to feel engaged, and know that you are with me on a journey to some unknown, where a worthy outcome awaits, while we walk the tightrope together, balancing between the thrill of success and the terror of failure. I want that deepest of human experiences with you—feeling connected, the two of us in full resonance, creating meaning together.

And, by the way, I want to create something with external value, too. Gallup says that the overall cost of disengagement to the U.S. economy is estimated to be $319 billion to $398 billion annually. Make money *and* have fun? Imagine that!

The leader's task, then, is to somehow make use of this wasted asset sitting in the room and convert it into vibrant participation. The problem is that only 18% of personnel are considered talented enough to be in a management role, according to Gallup. At some level, people long for liberation from their cocooned life. They yearn for a leader who will guide them out of their inertness and into active, creative expression that expresses who they are at their core. But when their leader cannot do that, they are disappointed once again and the vicious cycle repeats. Then, as we are reminded by the old adage: People don't leave their jobs, they leave their bosses.

STARTUP FAILURE: TODAY'S ESTIMATES OF STARTUP FAILURE RUN FROM 75% TO 90%

I am not surprised at these statistics from Gallup. Having been involved with literally scores of startups as founder, CEO, or adviser,

I have seen the endless ways in which failure comes about. Many of these involve factors that are staring us in the face, yet we cannot see them.

There are some recurring themes, though. One is that we behave more like *gamblers*, when we need to act more like growers. Instead of picking out the most attractive seedling in the nursery, we need to think more about preparing the ground, improving the atmosphere, and bathing it in the kind of light that promotes growth. Investors, with backgrounds oriented toward the financial and rational, do not seem to appreciate this need. Consequently, we revert to spray and pray. To date, it simply seems much easier to plant a bunch of stuff and hope for the best than to engage in the protracted and challenging task of nurturance over an extended period of time.

The *gambler* mindset is reflected in our metaphors. We place a bet, play the odds, put all our chips on a certain square, and hope to hit the jackpot. Yet, as this approach attracts more players, the marginal returns from the game diminish. Consequently, we see a trend away from institutional venture capital toward angel groups, full-service incubators, and accelerators that attempt to train the whole person. Meanwhile, the old guard sometimes seems stuck looking for luck in all the wrong places.

Another pattern of failure is a continued reliance on the solo hero model. I've always said that investors have a one-bit control mechanism while sitting on the board of startup: Hire or fire the CEO. This places the entire potential for success on a single individual and neglects the emerging trend of where the power resides in a team that is properly configured for creativity and execution. The selection process is biased toward charisma, eloquence, and aggressiveness, and does not know how to assess—much less engender—the leadership qualities leading to the preferred team outcome.

We need a better approach. As suggested in *The Archetypal Imagination* (Carolyn and Ernest Fay's Series in Analytical Psychology) in a slightly different context, leaders need to be "intuitives with a keen eye for the suggestive detail, the reading of the surface to intimate the implicit subtext or the layers of meaning which are embodied through the image but which are indiscernible to the sensate eye." Leaders are "obliged to read the surface of presentations and discern the hidden motives," along with the creative potential of the team unhampered by narcissism, egotism, and reductionist black-and-white thinking.

BUSINESS FAILURES ARE COMMON AND COSTLY

Familiar categories include:

- Mergers and acquisitions (~70% failure rate, according to McKinsey)
- Business process engineering (80% failure rate)
- Product introduction disasters: the 1957 Edsel, 1985's New Coke, Sony Betamax in 1975, 1993's Apple Newton, 1994's Commodore
- High-profile, often completely unexpected company implosions: 1991, Pan Am; 2001, Enron; 2002, WorldCom; 2002, Swiss Air; 2007, Bear Stearns; 2008, Lehman Brothers
- Dot-com crashes. One significant example from many: The grocery delivery startup Webvan, having raised $391M in venture capital funding, plus $375M from its 1999 initial public offering, collapsed in 2001, with its stock plummeting from $30 to $.06 a share.

Even this abbreviated list begs the following questions: Does business spend most of its time in failure mode? Why is failure such a common outcome? Are leadership practices and management theory inadequate? Or are we asking the wrong questions? Is the root cause of organizational dysfunctionality something else entirely?

To address these questions and others, a new type of leadership seems to be in the making. Let's take a look.

CHAPTER 4

INTIMATIONS OF A NEW LEADERSHIP MODEL

Creative Collaboration Is Profitable

Researchers from McKinsey published the 2006 paper *Competitive Advantage Through Better Interactions*. They purported to show a bottom-line advantage to managing what they call "tacit activities"—interactions we refer to as creative collaboration or transformative dialogue. They segregated industries into those requiring a low, medium, or high level of creativity. Not all industries require high levels of creativity; mining is one such example they identify. Digging stuff out of the ground involves challenges similar in every mine. Standardization to eliminate variability and reduce costs is the primary mandate. On the other hand, high technology concerns inventing new technologies and products. This is all about creativity.

McKinsey's researchers then examined average earnings before interest, tax, depreciation, and amortization (EBITDA) per employee in each industry (see Figure 4-1). Mining ranged from $2,000 to $248,000. Hence, those in the mining business probably are not losing money and could be making almost a quarter of a million dollars

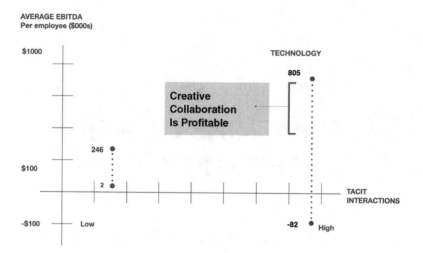

FIGURE 4-1   McKinsey Shows Creative Collaboration Is Profitable

per employee. However, in industries requiring a high level of creativity, such as high-tech, EBITDA per employee covers a much broader range: from a loss of $62,000 to a profit of $805,000. The latter number makes venture capitalists happy; the former often drives them to drink.

Now McKinsey's bottom line, as it were, is that *companies able to sustain creative collaboration well are in the upper quartile of EBITDA per employee.*

In fact, in explaining their results, the researchers wrote "Companies that make tacit activities [a.k.a., creative collaboration] more productive will not only raise top and bottom lines but also build talent-based competitive advantages that rivals will find hard to match." Further, they wrote that "tacit interactions reduce the importance of structure and elevate the importance of people and collaboration."

This report marks a relatively stunning moment in American management consulting history: McKinsey, one of the most prominent icons of rational, quantitative, hard-nosed analysis, establishes an empirical link between a "soft practice" (creative collaboration) and the bottom line. It also contains a bigger meaning: the old, top-down hierarchical mindset encounters the new collaborative, open, more network-centric approach.

SAFETY FIRST

Educators have stressed the importance of psychological safety for decades. In short, unless one feels safe, one cannot effectively address the tasks of learning. Recently, Laszlo Bock, Google's head of People Operations (Human Resources to non-Googlers) undertook a study focused on team dynamics, hoping to determine what distinguishes the most successful teams. Bock had thought the study would reveal "the perfect mix of individual traits and skills necessary for a stellar team." Instead, the conclusion was that "Who is on a team matters less than how the team members interact, structure their work, and view their contributions." Of 250 dynamics considered and reviewed, psychological safety topped the list of the five most significant traits, by a wide margin. So wide that it's considered to be "the underpinnings" of the other four traits: dependability, structure and clarity, meaning, and purpose.

What is psychological safety? Harvard Business School professor Amy Edmondson defines it as "a shared belief that the team is safe for interpersonal risk taking." And how is it important? As Julia Rozovsky, Analyst, Google People Operations, wrote in her blog: "Individuals on teams with higher psychological safety are less likely to leave Google, they're more likely to harness the power of diverse ideas from their teammates, they bring in more revenue, and they're rated as effective twice as often by executives." Establishing a sense of psychological safety—ensuring that team members can take risks without feeling insecure or embarrassed—requires effort. How, for instance, do you make certain that employees will not worry that questions or suggestions they raise will reveal to others that they are "out of the loop" (a fate that's worrisome in any organization, potentially more so in tech)?

Other conversations include a thorough exposition of the value of partnering, what the author and colleagues have been promoting for more than a decade. This conversation reinforces what we call "Twinning" in this book. While that treatment provides a thorough taxonomy of modes of partnering, we dig deeper into the archetypal and mythic layer in support of the practice. Other discussions emphasize the principle of connectedness in the new leadership, where we go further into the how-to aspects of implementing that approach.

Notice the prevalence of new language: creative collaboration, psychological safety, partnering, connectedness, etc., suggesting new language and a new narrative about leadership.

TEAM OF TEAMS

When I presented *Blueprint* to Richard Adler, the highly distinguished Fellow of the Institute for the Future in Palo Alto and former *Wall Street Journal* editor, he mentioned that the highest profile example of using this methodology was provided by General Stanley McChrystal as reported in his book *Team of Teams*. Upon my immediate review of the book, I was astonished. First, it is an engrossing and extremely readable account of a very important part of our national defense infrastructure. Second, and most striking to me, is the close parallel between his account of a transformational leadership process and the themes and methods described in this book.

The story begins with McChrystal assuming command of the Joint Special Operations Task Force (the "Task Force") around 2003. The team was up against Al Qaeda in Iraq (AQI) and discovered a different kind of opponent. AQI was a highly decentralized and unorthodox structure, unlike the traditional military hierarchical approach developed by the U.S. over centuries. The task force eventually realized that AQI was extremely proficient in "resilience": the ability to take hits and still maintain its overall functioning. AQI also made effective use of social media in its network structure. The task force found itself up against an enemy that, according to traditional thinking, it should've dominated, and yet they were losing. They needed to change.

The overall approach was to create a culture and system based on extremely transparent information sharing, coupled with decentralized decision-making authority, something called "Empowered Execution." This placed a strong emphasis on horizontal cross-functional collaboration as a complementary approach to the traditional vertical command and control structure of the military. To defeat a network, they realized that the Task Force would have to become a new network. A key innovation of *Team of Teams* is that each team had a representative from another team, opposed to the impossible approach that each team member knew every member of other teams. He also instituted the daily Operations & Intelligence (O&I) briefing with eventually up to 7,000 people attending for up to two hours. This practice enabled all members of the organization to see the big picture in real time and gave them the skills and confidence to solve their own problems without the need for further guidance and clarification. The results were astonishing. In particular, the Task Force could go from only a few sorties a day to hundreds.

The parallels between *Team of Teams* and this book are multiple. McChrystal's book talks about "shared consciousness," and this book describes a similar concept in the "superior creativity and intelligence of the connected team." *Team of Teams* describes the effect on creativity and performance due to full information sharing and empowered execution. He places a critical role of trust in the team as described in my book *Built on Trust* (2000) and elaborated subsequently in multiple texts. We describe how creative collaboration in a safe, high-trust environment can lead to superior results otherwise unattainable. He also describes the horizontal (versus traditional vertical, hierarchical) dimensions of collaboration, an instance of complementarity we will develop much further in this book. McChrystal also revises the role of the leader from the solo hero approach, which this book rejects, to the overall "gardener" style of management already mentioned.

We believe that *Team of Teams* is a huge contribution to determining the new model of leadership. Its inclusion of multiple interesting stories reinforces the power of McChrystal's description of the new leadership model. In some ways, this book is complementary to *Team of Teams*. We focus on business and startup environments, while he deals with a military application. He provides more interesting stories than this single author could possibly compile, while we go further into the how-to aspects of execution practices, He identifies trust, common purpose, shared consciousness, and empowered execution as the basis for superior performance. We break that down further into three underlying principles and four operational practices. We also go after the hidden factors that, often unacknowledged, drive outcome. He, too, accesses the mythic layer in his description of Proteus as the underlying archetypal figure behind AQI as a present manifestation. We also do an extensive recitation of the mythic layer, including about six different ancient figures, in terms of their implications for leadership. As a final humorous point, I have for decades been talking about Taylor as a critical turning point for the development of the machine-model management style in business in the twentieth century. He goes further and tells the full story of Taylor, reinforcing the emergence of the Taylor method as a signpost toward a leadership approach that is increasingly obsolete.

CHAPTER 5

THE NEW MODEL OF LEADERSHIP

A Network, Not a Hierarchy

The new leadership model is radically different from the hierarchical model of the past. It appears to be more of a network than a traditional organization chart (Figure 5-1).

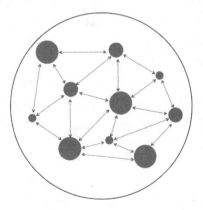

FIGURE 5-1 Network Model

In this network, some nodes are larger than others, reflecting the reality that some participants on the team have greater responsibilities or deeper skills than others. The links between nodes represent not reporting relationships, but deep communication paths enabling radically open communication in a high-trust environment. Creative collaboration is the central organizing principle for the new model, delivering on the promise of the superior intelligence and creativity of the connected team. What follows is access to the deep imagination at the individual and team level, resulting in acute perception sparking inventive ideas, inspired content, and unique visions. As global competitive pressures drive the search for competitive advantage, we now look to the connected team as a solution, immediately available to the inspired leader.

The term "deep imagination" may at first glance seem peculiar. However, deep imagination has already been in play and been demonstrated in many enterprises. For example, at one point in time, George Lucas reached into the imaginative layer and created *Star Wars*. Likewise, Elon Musk imagined the benefits of commercial space travel and created SpaceX, and followed a similar process with Tesla.

Dr. Joseph Cambray, CEO of Pacifica Graduate Institute, sheds more light on this network model based on his research. He suggests that an "Emerging Global Structure" comes into existence as a result of the network topology. This structure has certain properties that depend not on the properties of the individual nodes but *wholly on the nature of their interactions*. An example in chemistry involves the mystery of why water is not a gas at room temperature. After all, hydrogen sulfide (H_2S) is a gas at room temperature, with sulfur at a molecular weight of 32μ, and water (H_2O) includes oxygen at a molecular weight one-half that of sulfur at 16μ. Based on the properties of these two compounds, water would have to be a gas at room temperature. But those *properties* do not determine collective behavior; it is the nature of the *interactions* between the compounds that make that determination.

The network model defines the future path to high-performance, creative organizations. *Blueprint* delivers on this model with authentic impact.

REALIZING THE NEW MODEL

An immediate question is "How do we make this new model a reality in my organization?" First, understand that migration to this open system may require a deep transformation of the existing culture and mindset. One cannot simply say, "We are now an open organization starting tomorrow." You can't just jump to the answer. The leadership has to be unconditionally committed to this approach and be willing to go the distance to make it happen. And each organization will have its unique and often peculiar challenges to overcome. Later, we will discuss potential issues in implementation, including resistance and confusion, and ultimately recognition and celebration. In the meantime, there is no cheap grace here, but rather a purposeful effort sustained over time.

THE CREATIVE FRONTIER: ENLARGING OUR MENTAL CAPACITY

Blueprint places a consistent emphasis on creativity as the new frontier for discovering competitive advantage. Where does that creativity come from? Admonishing teams to "be creative" isn't going to do it. Instead, the approach is to create an environment that allows creativity to emerge spontaneously. One might then argue that there is little more there than what conventional thinking suggests, and the search might be futile. But consider another perspective.

The moniker Milky Way Brain comes from the observation that the number of neurons in the human brain is the same as the number of stars in the Milky Way: 100 billion. Betsy Burroughs points out that the Milky Way Brain has an enormous potential for innovation and insight. She argues that our thinking brain, the prefrontal cortex, can only handle about four items at a time (try this test: add two- or three-digit numbers in your head quickly) and tires in a short period of time. On the other hand, neural pathways can process thoughts in the background all the time (hence, the experience of "waking up thoughts"). The problem is that those background or subliminal tasks can easily be drowned out when we are "freaked out or worried or upset. Because when we are, that's 'high signal noise' in our brain and it drowns out any awareness we might have of a new insight or solution."

This provides a striking confirmation of the approach in this book: Reduce distracting drama—including the inner noise of our own egos seeking attention—to better access, on both an individual and team level, more creative brain processes. The approach is reminiscent of Michelangelo's (probably apocryphal) statement about how he sculpted the famous statue of David: "It [was] easy. You just chip away the stone that doesn't look like David." By removing the ambient noise, you can more easily detect the signal.

Another way to think about enlarging our mental capacity is to consider that we have two minds: the rational mind and the imaginative mind. The rational mind is dominated by the ego, with its superior intelligence, but also encumbered by idealized fantasies, the will to dominate, and self-centeredness. The rational mind likes to "figure things out" and thinks it is in control. The imaginative mind operates from a deeper layer and has an autonomous nature. (Of course, many creative people also have huge egos that operate in parallel with the imaginative mind.) That is, it can generate ideas that surprise us, and sometimes we wake up in the morning wondering "Where did that come from?" The autonomous imagination can provide, as it were, feedstock in the form of images, connections, thoughts, and intuitions to the conscious mind for further development and elaboration. One of the areas for research is how technology—virtual and augmented reality, online collaboration, social interaction, etc.—can further the activity of the autonomous imagination. Meanwhile, the culture defined by *Blueprint* liberates individuals to more deeply access their creative selves and also provides the team environment that collaboratively processes the combined set of individual contributions into an integrated whole.

TOWARD LEADERSHIP CONSCIOUSNESS: CREATIVE CAPACITY

Our intention in this book is to encourage a deeper consciousness in leadership. A major problem of discussing consciousness—and there are many such problems—is unconsciousness of consciousness. People view our thought patterns and modes of perception as the entirety of our existence. Not so. A common dream pattern may illustrate the point. In this dream, you are in your house or a location familiar to you. Suddenly you become aware of a door that wasn't there before, leading to a whole new area of the house. Your reaction is one of amazement. "Where did this come from?" "Why didn't I know about this before?" If you take the house in the dream as a symbol of the self, the dream suggests you are not so much a familiar house of seven rooms but rather a mansion of possibility, and your task is to move in and take possession of the residence.

Your mind is telling you that you have a greater capacity than you think you do.

Metaphorically speaking, discovering new rooms may be likened to discovering new solutions. That is, the mind has a certain plasticity that can be utilized in creativity (as C.G. Jung wrote in *The Secret of the Golden Flower*):

> I always worked with the temperamental conviction that in the last analysis there are no insoluble problems, and experience has so far justified me in that I have often seen individuals who simply outgrew a problem which had destroyed others. This "outgrowing," as I called it previously, revealed itself on further experience to be the raising of the level of consciousness. Some higher or wider interest arose on the person's horizon, and

through this widening of his view, the insoluble problem lost its urgency. It was not solved logically in its own terms, but faded out in contrast to a new and stronger life-tendency.

This doesn't mean we all need years of therapy (although probably everybody could benefit from some). We do need to connect openly to other team members while keeping our personal egos as unattached as possible during that process. Multiple parties engaged with an issue will tend to converge on an accurate perspective, compensating and correcting individual error. Hence, the "wisdom of teams (or crowds)," and hence the use of consensus facilitates the superior insight of the connected team without abandoning decision-making. Multiple perspectives need not result in organizational anarchy and chaos.

CHAPTER 6

BLUEPRINT: DELIVERING THE NEW MODEL

Leadership Journey from Innovation to Execution

The *Blueprint* system architecture is shown in Figure 6-1.

The bottom layer, Principles, includes empathy, complementarity, and nonattachment. These principles (which in time become habits of mind) provide the foundation for creative collaboration. Complementarity—the notion of always this *and* that, not this *or* that—is a crucial, yet often unrecognized, leadership trait. Complementarity is embedded throughout our approach in its attempt to grasp the inherent paradox of both/and thinking. In a manner to be described, complementarity plays a key role in enabling creative dialogue. Empathy, which is by now broadly recognized as an important leadership skill, has remained in need of a method for implementation. We provide it and describe throughout the book how to *do* empathy, enabling connection. The third habit—nonattachment—is the ability to avoid those weird and stubborn flights of

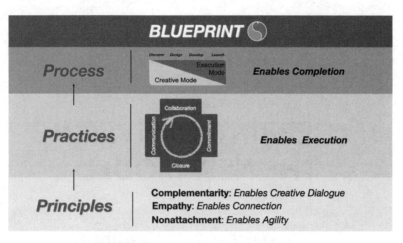

FIGURE 6-1   The Blueprint Architecture

fantasy that possess leaders and take them down strange and some-times disastrous paths. Nonattachment addresses the need to avoid biases, attachments, and idealized fantasies in our creative dialogue, thereby enabling agility.

These three principles take our conversation from the logical, where much of business dialogue resides, to the *psycho*logical where motive, action, and meaning lie. As David "Doc" Searls, co-author of *The Cluetrain Manifesto* and author of *The Intention Economy*, suggests, "Reason sits on life's board of directors, but emotion casts the final vote." We ignore emotion at our own peril and put our organizations in peril at the same time by doing so.

These principles drive performance. Complementarity estab-lishes a condition of "one mind" in the team. Empathy glues the team together in creative dialogue. And nonattachment clears the path to a shared common view that would otherwise be blocked by dialogue-ending fixed positions. With these principles in place, cre-ativity can blossom. The connected team effectively becomes multiple interconnected minds, each with its own access to the deeper layers of the intuitive mind and, in turn, more effective collaboration. The combined effect is to open and gain access to a vast range of creative resources advantageous to the search for competitive advantage.

The middle layer prescribes four Practices, where execution resides: Collaboration, Commitment, Closure, and Communication. While these practices sound familiar and ordinary, in fact effective implementation is more of an art form, and we will describe hard-earned methods for successful implementation of each.

The top layer describes Process, with the explicit intent to provide a full life-cycle approach that goes from Discover through Design, Develop, and Launch. The creation of this process was motivated to correct the frequent problem of teams generating great designs that never get turned into products. As we will see, a foundational aspect of the process is the managed transition from the creative mindset to the execution mindset, already an example of complementarity in action in this book.

We also employ a three-layer *diagnostic model* that illuminates the hidden factors that enable high-performance teams.

In total—the combination of the principles described earlier, and the four key practices of communication and the three-layer diagnostic model—constitute *Blueprint*, a superior "Execution System." As mentioned before, the diagnostic model defines the What we seek to optimize, the three principles define the Why, and the four key practices define the How.

This approach may seem complex, but it can actually be understood and implemented in a short period of time. We liken it to the game of Go, where simple rules can be learned quickly, and then performance continues to improve over time with practice and experience. The constituent elements of the implementation system compress decades of trial-and-error experience into a short learning cycle, enabling you to reach a high level of proficiency far more efficiently.

MYTH AND THE HERO'S JOURNEY

Myths are to cultures like dreams are to individuals: They capture over-arching critical themes, offer insights, and sometimes provide solutions. And have for much of the span of time. More: Myths are considered a "mega power tool" and "story is medicine." And business is just a story in a new guise. Jung has written that what man is, when viewed in relation to the eternal, "can only be expressed by way of myth. Myth is more individual and expresses life more precisely than does science. Science works with concepts of averages which are far too general to do justice to the subjective variety of an individual life." Myths also entertain us, taking us into the precincts of mystery. In a more recent context, we will see how Dr. Kwame Scruggs uses myths to rescue inner city youth, say-ing "Myths are false on the outside, but true on the inside. Stories that have never been, but are always true. They are not just to put children to sleep, but to wake up adults. Ideas enlighten the mind; stories touch the soul."

We begin our exploration of leadership at the mythic layer by examining Joseph Campbell's *The Hero's Journey*. While this topic has received a great deal of attention recently and we need not repeat all its applications here, we will take a little extra time here studying it, given its pathway to the mythic layer with its abundant instructions for team life today.

As you can imagine, the Director of the Mythological Studies Program at Pacifica Graduate Institute, Lans Smith, knows more than a bit about mythology. The introduction to his very accessible book, *The Complete Idiot's Guide to World Mythology*, explains that one way to understand the truth of mythology is to:

> Consider the myth of the "Boy Who Cried Wolf." ... Chances are no such incident ever happened. We tell this to children to understand that habitual lying makes it hard for people to believe you when you are telling the truth. So ... the story is one of truth, whether or not it is actually fact. Fact doesn't matter, as it has no effect whatsoever on the value of a myth.

Now, you might think of The Boy Who Cried Wolf as a fairy tale or a fable (thank you, Aesop) to guide children. True enough. And depending upon its telling, the consequences for the boy are moral (when he truly does need help, no one believes him) or mortal (in some versions, the wolf eats not just the sheep but also the boy). But myth? The story itself can be traced back to classical times and continues to speak to us. Enough to put it in the mythic category.

Joseph Campbell studied stories across all cultures, including myths, fairy tales, fables, and contemporary literature, seeking their universal structure and purpose. The pattern (the "monomyth") he discovered and wrote of in *The Hero with a Thousand Faces* describes stages in the narrative of a hero's quest, his experiences along the way, and his return to the community from which he started. Campbell's work has been applied to an immense body of literature, popularized through multiple publications, and elucidated in Bill Moyer's PBS broadcasts, *The Power of Myth*.

Indeed, myths are everywhere, including popular culture. George Lucas acknowledged the influence of myth in general (and of Campbell in particular) on *Star Wars*. Other examples include Dorothy in *The Wizard of Oz*, Bilbo Baggins in *The Hobbit*, and Simba at Pride Rock in *The Lion King*. Indeed, the influence of the patterns

Campbell identified can be seen almost everywhere. Script-writing courses at UCLA and other institutions have been described as "all about Freud, Jung, and Campbell."

In addition to its application to the immense body of classical mythology and literature, the Hero's Journey can be applied at the microlevel in business. When we are initiating a new product development project, launching a startup, or simply developing a new promotional program, we are entering into a process distilled by Campbell. Let's illustrate the startup process with his four-stage, model: the Call, the Departure, Helpers Along the Way, and the Return.

THE CALL

In the coffee houses, fitness centers, and restaurants of Silicon Valley, someone with a concept for a startup is excitedly (and confidentially) describing it to a trusted colleague or friend. This could be idle chatter. But in some cases, a passionate visionary genuinely feels and then pursues the high-tech version of The Call.

In fairy tales, it is easy to spot The Call, whether it is the momma pig telling her children it is time for them to go build their own houses, or Hansel and Gretel overhearing their parents plan their abandonment, or Little Red Riding Hood hearing about her sickly grandmother and deciding to take cake and wine to her. Should we get The Call, we must decide what to do about it. Has this occurred in your life? What happened? Did you heed the Call and, if so, where did it lead? Or did you decline it, and how does that now look in retrospect?

The Call can be a critical moment in life. It could open the doors to expansive experiences and acquired meaning. It also suggests a downside: Campbell famously said "If you refuse the Call, you become a victim to be rescued." Look around; you may see how this has operated in your life or in other people's lives.

THE DEPARTURE

Anyone who accepts the Call enters an unknown (Campbell's "Belly of the Whale") domain characterized by risk and uncertainty. "The adventure is always and everywhere a passage beyond the veil of the known into the unknown ... yet for anyone *with competence and courage the danger fades*," Campbell wrote in *The Hero with a Thousand Faces*. The practices in this book will help you navigate through this phase. By tapping creative collaboration, you will open to a wider and deeper range of solutions. And by recognizing and avoiding idealized expectations (all too often idealized fantasies), you can maintain a degree of detachment and a capacity for dialogue that supports creativity and leads to innovation.

The three hazards early in the journey are impatience, despair, and false teachings.

Impatience

In my experience, the very early stage of a startup involves an immense amount of dialogue. Converting a new concept into a coherent interplay of technology, marketing, and financial management requires sustained effort. The incremental effort required to define the organizational culture necessary to implement your vision now, rather than later when problems emerge, will pay off handsomely. Yet it conflicts with the impulse to "get going" as expeditiously as possible. Resist the impulse and the impatience motivating it.

Despair

In one company, where we needed to do research for a potential product, I pulled the team together to attack the problem. I warned them at the outset of a three-day offsite meeting that there may be moments of despair. The typical offsite experience is U-shaped: starting out high, descending into frustration, then ending on another high note. A day into the offsite meeting, after we had successfully laid out a strategy and product roadmap, the collective dialogue unearthed a basic flaw:

Customers really didn't want that product! Silence descended. Then one of the engineers said, "Is this the moment of despair you were talking about?" My response to her was simple: "Yes, it is. Now let's find a better solution." We did—and it later turned out to be our "killer product." One might feel that we had wasted our first day. We hadn't. Instead, that day's work, leading to the unpleasant realization of no market for our initial product idea, saved us from six months of what would have been wasted effort and simultaneously opened the door to what became instead a successful product launch.

False Teachings (Bad Advice)

Many inexperienced entrepreneurs, especially those with freshly minted MBAs, believe effectiveness scales with elegance. They may come up with elaborate plans that are simply not workable. Overly optimistic or outright inflated expectations of quick and easy success require constant vigilance to avoid having the project sidetracked or derailed. Financial investors can provide important guidance to inexperienced teams. That's a plus. But that guidance can also burden a new enterprise with outdated ideas and the baggage and fallout of bad experiences from previous ventures.

All three of these hazards—impatience, despair, and false teachings—are related to idealized expectations (more thoroughly described in Chapter 22). This phase depends more on intuition than on ego. Try to stay in the flow of practical problem-solving and not overthink things.

HELPERS ALONG THE WAY

During the Hero's Journey, crucial assistance frequently comes from unexpected quarters. Think how often Han Solo appears out of nowhere at critical junctures in the Star Wars movies. Obi-Wan Kenobi and then Yoda offer to mentor Luke Skywalker. Unconditional commitment to a cause inspires a response: Other people want to help. Moreover, when one's commitment is visceral and unconditional—not just intellectual and affected—resources show up in all kinds of circumstances, happy coincidences, and plain luck.

I have often had helpers from outside the board-management team show up to provide critical support. These included a senior industry executive guiding me through a challenging company sales process, a former senior defense department official making key introductions, and an expert in time-based competition helping to establish an effective product development program. These encounters seem to arise when you focus on a task or mission intensely yet remain receptive to unforeseen assistance.

THE RETURN

The process of bringing an innovation to life also encounters typical challenges. One of the classic challenges identified by Campbell is the Hero's refusal to return. In startups, this may be seen in unending efforts to improve a product and in resistance to releasing it in its current form. The concept of a minimum viable product (MVP) released for early customer feedback can be viewed as a corrective to this common tendency to resist returning from the adventure of product development to the mundane business tasks no less important to organizational success.

Multiple cycles of this type can occur both sequentially and in parallel throughout the life of an enterprise. The Hero's Journey archetype is a useful roadmap to understand the process and deepen the team's faith in its ability to meet commitments and achieve goals.

Blueprint is the Hero's Journey, with its call, departure, negotiation through the creative process, and the return to deliver the benefit.

PART II

Diagnostic System

The What of Leadership

CHAPTER 7

THE HIDDEN TO
BE REVEALED

That Which Is Not Acknowledged
Rules Outcome

To get to those hidden factors described in Chapter 1, we need a map—a schematic that exposes the underlying layers where those factors cower in the dark, conspiring interference. This will take a deep dive into those limiting character traits—as James Madison wrote in *The Federalist Papers*: "sown in the nature of man." Over the next few chapters, we will describe a three-layer model that we have found useful in separating the various sets of factors into distinct categories. We will describe each layer in detail, including its essential elements. This model explicitly recognizes that there are separate layers interacting at the same time. And it provides a useful diagnostic tool for understanding your environment and identifying root causes in need of remediation.

For much of its history, formal MBA training programs have attributed such failures to flaws in business strategy or operations. The underlying (and usually unacknowledged) assumption is that the correct application of the skills instilled in MBAs—finance, accounting, engineering, manufacturing, marketing, and strategy—suffice for business success. If you do x, y, and z, then you will succeed. Failure implies that you didn't do your homework. The MBA model assumes a top layer in the overall Enterprise, where leadership decisions, and the organizational implementation of those decisions, determine business outcomes. (See Figure 7-1.)

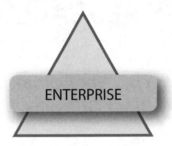

FIGURE 7-1   The Enterprise Layer

But how well do the concepts taught in business schools apply to business practice? Consider one typical startup failure: developing a product with a low sales price to attract customers but that also requires a direct sales force to reach prospects. Because a direct sales force is probably the most expensive distribution approach, the average selling price (ASP) must be high enough to compensate for selling costs. However, a price high enough to justify direct sales limits the sales volume to less than what the business needs to survive. The result? Enterprise failure.

The obvious conclusion is that the business team failed to do their homework. Rationally, and with hindsight, we can see that the ASP needed to be significantly higher to justify the cost of a direct sales force.

But there is something incomplete about this explanation, too. Much as we would all like a straight line to success, business depends on much more than numbers. Sometimes, even with meticulous planning, and all the right intentions and strategies in place, things just seem to fall apart. Sometimes outcomes are not commensurate with effort.

Between the plans and the postmortems exists the underlying culture in which day-to-day business operations take place. Within this layer, the standard business bromide, "There just wasn't enough buy-in," rings true. The culture of each business decisively, yet usually unconsciously, shapes not only routine business operations but overall business strategy. (See Figure 7-2.)

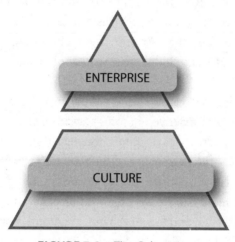

FIGURE 7-2   The Culture Layer

By Culture Layer we mean the actual, *de facto* customs, rules, and patterns of behavior that are in play among team members. It includes all interactions—one-to-one, one-to-many, many-to-many—and incorporates how well people relate to each other within the organization. These rules and patterns may be explicit and purposefully promoted, perhaps even aspirational.

Or, as is far more often the case, the rules and patterns may be automatic and unconscious. These are the ingrained organizational habits. A few examples:

- Do people tell the truth in their business interactions?
- Are people comfortable raising questions?
- Do people withhold information or dissemble about uncomfortable facts?

- Do people honor commitments?
- Are people willing to admit mistakes or report slippage?
- Do people trust each other?
- Is the team unified around a common vision?
- Are there common instances of "Them versus Us"?

The cultural patterns in an organization can be healthy, pathological, or somewhere in between. Business culture is extraordinarily important, even more than strategy. The Culture Layer may contain many, if not most, of the hidden factors that drive business success or failure.

What is the root cause of the culture in place for a particular organization? Culture derives, in some way, from leadership. In many organizations (and perhaps disproportionately in startups), the culture simply resembles the personality of the founder(s), however peculiar, eccentric, unbalanced, constructive, or inspiring. And future outcome can be readily traced back to the organization's characteristic mindset.

The Mindset Layer refers to the inner contours, both intellectual and emotional, of the people responsible for team creation and leadership. The diagnostic challenge within the Mindset Layer varies in accordance with different manifestations of organizational dysfunction. (See Figure 7-3.)

HOW THE MODEL WORKS: BOTTOM-UP PROGRESSION DRIVES PERFORMANCE

It is probably inarguable that good strategy is critical to success. It is, as argued in the Preface, a necessary condition. Our argument is that it is not sufficient, and that the quality of leadership is the determinative factor. Hence, this model proceeds in a bottom-up fashion as shown in Figure 7-4.

Competent mindset, in turn, creates an effective culture with a corresponding execution ability. Leaders don't perform execution; the team does. Then culture sets up the organization for performance.

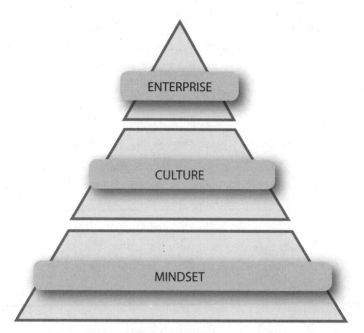

FIGURE 7-3   The Three-Layer Model

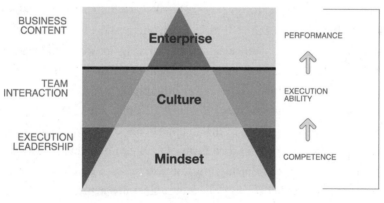

FIGURE 7-4   Bottom-Up Progression

This model exposes the role of Mindset in driving culture. While there seems to be a widespread appreciation for the power of culture, there also appears to be a lack of understanding of what culture really means. Our conversations are filled with bromides like "Go for it" or "No politics" or "Be passionate." All true, and all equally useless in telling us how to develop a clear culture. Yet the recognized importance of culture persists, and many emphasize its importance by repeating that "Culture eats strategy for lunch."

The keys to creating an effective culture lie in the Mindset Layer. Misalignment between mindset and culture leads to the all-too-frequent case where the behavior in the room bears no resemblance to the code of ethics on the wall. Authentic culture must reflect who the company and its personnel are authentically. Going through the intellectual process of specifying the culture without understanding underlying mindset is like building a structure starting on the second floor. So, we add: "Mindset eats culture for breakfast."

To understand the Mindset Layer further, let's look at its essential dimensions.

DIMENSIONS OF MINDSET: THE ARCHETYPAL, UNDERLYING PATTERNS OF MINDSET

Figure 7-5 exposes the four archetypal ("original model or prototype") dimensions of the Mindset Layer. Archetypal in the sense that they are underlying, universal factors driving mindset. Experience has validated that understanding where an organization resides along these dimensions provides a powerful, and often definitive, assessment of its capability to support a strong culture and thereby execute it. Dozens of applications of this diagnostic model have provided useful direction for action and confirm our observation that discussions of culture without understanding mindset is an intellectual exercise without material benefit as to how organizations actually perform.

Each of these dimensions has a dual, or complementary, aspect, typically along intellectual versus emotional dimensions. Courage includes the capacity to take bold and fearless action in the marketplace, but also to be willing to hear and process unwelcome input from the team that could have a redeeming effect on organizational outcome.

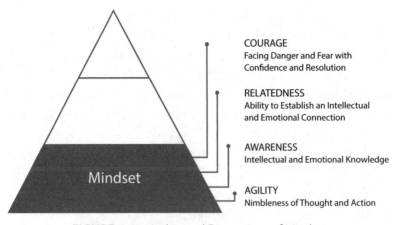

COURAGE
Facing Danger and Fear with
Confidence and Resolution

RELATEDNESS
Ability to Establish an Intellectual
and Emotional Connection

AWARENESS
Intellectual and Emotional Knowledge

AGILITY
Nimbleness of Thought and Action

FIGURE 7-5   Archetypal Dimensions of Mindset

Relatedness, a seemingly later arrival in cultural discussions, implies an intellectual understanding of staying connected with customers, but also insists on respecting the emotional connections across the team. Awareness implies a thorough understanding of the company's markets, technologies, and strategies. It also implies a close understanding of the emotional life of the team and whether or not the principles and practices in this book are being adhered to. Finally, Agility includes the capacity to have a buttoned-down product development program and then turn on a dime when it's discovered it's going in the wrong direction. It also includes the ability to listen to another person's point of view without outright, dogmatic rejection due to its incompatibility with your currently biased position.

The very dimensions of Mindset therefore include understanding the principle of complementarity as a basis for *Blueprint*, as is covered later in this book.

Example: Mindset Sabotages Outcome

I learned in business school that 80% of industry outcomes can be forecasted by a thorough analysis of market, competition, channels, and economic factors. A premise of this book is that it should be possible to predict future business outcomes over a period of several years by the appropriate measurement of current Mindset and Culture Layers. This would introduce a new type of predictive analytics, anchored more deeply in the underlying factors actually driving outcomes.

Imagine that we had the leadership equivalent of eagle vision and could see problems above and below the water line—and address them effectively. The following is a cautionary tale to help improve our keen vision.

In one early-stage software company, a board member and investor proclaimed: "The first-year revenue is $10M … or else!" A dramatic statement, certainly. The investor had a grandiose ego, immediately apparent in even a brief conversation.

Saying "The first-year revenue is $10M … or else!" discounted or outright ignored reality: Software companies need products to secure revenue, and developing software products takes time. Together with the implied threat of "or else," those few words (repeated often) created a cultural reaction that included creating forbidden topics ("That's impossible"). That threat also forced dissent to go underground, which naturally generated toxic gossip (because dissent is irrepressible in nature) and created a disastrous culture of forced commitments. In the ensuing dumb show of playing out the fantasy, irresponsible actions were undertaken. These included building out the organization at substantial cost to support a revenue ramp that simply was not feasible.

The bottom-up nature of this real-world example is illustrated in Figure 7-6.

Not an organization conducive to a cohesive and unified workforce. And that's just one example of many.

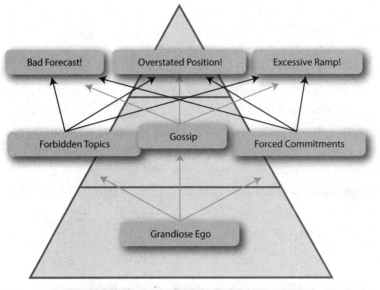

FIGURE 7-6 Layer One Issues Migrate Upward

UNDERSTANDING THE FOUR DIMENSIONS: A BRIEF DIGRESSION

Depth psychologist Carl Jung's typology at the individual level can help us understand the Mindset Layer. He identified four aspects of personality, or psychological functions, in two opposing pairs. One pair consists of *thinking* and *feeling*; the other pair consists of *intuition* and *sensation*. Because thinking and feeling assess meaning and value, Jung called them rational because they function as a means of judgment. Intuition and sensation notice what exists or could exist; Jung called them irrational because they function as a means of perception (without judgment).

Thinking provides an intellectual basis for analysis. It prefers abstractions. Feeling provides an emotional basis for decisions. It determines the appropriate action for a specific situation. Thinking and feeling cannot function simultaneously. Thinking requires undistracted concentration, and too much thinking interferes with feeling.

Feeling involves immediate reactions, and too much feeling interferes with thinking. Because thinking and feeling are opposing functions, most people rely on one more than the other.

Intuition is concerned with possibilities that are not yet real, while sensation deals with the concrete here and now. Intuition looks inward, while sensation engages the senses. Intuition and sensation cannot function simultaneously. Intuition gropes toward unrealized possibilities, and too much sensation interferes with intuition. Sensation embraces the here and now, and too much intuition interferes with sensation. Because intuition and sensation are opposing functions, most people rely on one more than the other.

Hence, we can visualize these four functions in the relationship suggested by the diagram in Figure 7-7.

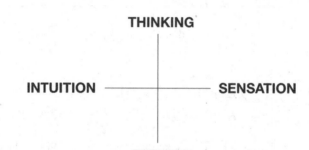

FIGURE 7-7 Jung's Typology

We all have one default function, what Jung called our *superior function*. This is what comes naturally, and what determines our outlook and behavior. (Mine happens to be thinking.) The opposing function languishes and becomes what Jung called our *inferior function*. (In my case, feeling.) The inferior function is a serious matter. As Jung put it, "You do not have an inferior function, it has you." This is where we feel out of control, incompetent, fumbling, and confused. It is also where the greatest potential resides for personal development.

THE INFERIOR DIMENSION: FAILURE COMES FROM THE WEAKEST DIMENSION OF MINDSET

Now, let's introduce Jung's psychological typology into our teamwork and leadership discussion. Just as a healthy body provides a defense against myriad possible diseases, so a balanced state among these four Mindset dimensions provides a defense against organizational dysfunction. The inferior Mindset dimension is the gateway for dysfunctionality to penetrate. At the same time, it offers the highest potential for the organization. For example, a team was stuck in the process of making a fundamental product development decision for *six months*. Clearly, their inferior dimension was Courage—in this case, courage to make a product decision, get the product out, and determine its viability. The members of the team were afraid of making a mistake, and their lack of courage caused dysfunctional behavior, such as gossip, blame shifting, and, obviously, schedule slippage. Their dysfunctional behavior cost their firm market leadership.

Another celebrated startup failed on all four dimensions. The CEO was appropriately passionate about her vision and was able to recruit credible partners and investors. However, she would also overreact when anyone raised concerns or expressed doubt about the direction of the firm. And there was no shortage of concerns and doubts. The company was badly organized and lacked scalable processes. Multiple areas of concern deserved attention. Unfortunately, the CEO's habit of berating dissenters cut off the exact type of dialogue that might have led to solutions. So … Lack of relatedness. Check. Lack of agility. Check. Lack of courage. Check. Lack of awareness. Check.

CHAPTER 8

MINDSET MALWARE

Leadership Dysfunction Is Common and Often Unrecognized

et's start with the messier, darker, and uncomfortable part of the Culture Layer rooted in the Mindset Layer. Most leadership is oblivious or indifferent to these organizational depths. Some leaders specialize in generating a specific type of maladjustment and raise its expression to an art form, while others gather multiple maladjustments into a pungent bouquet of sheer incompetence.

Undoubtedly, Figure 8-1 contains only a partial list, but it is verifiable. It includes Mindset malware we've encountered more than a few times over the years. It is also worthwhile at this point to share Scott Peck's admonition in his book *In Search of Stones* that all symptoms are overdetermined, meaning they can be traced to more than one root cause.

FIGURE 8-1   Examples of Mindset Malware

OVERCOMING MINDSET MALWARE

Identifying Mindset malware is relatively easy, once you know what to look for. Remedying the resultant symptoms, however, is far from easy because people tend to obsessively and compulsively repeat their bad habits. Too often, what you see is not only what you get—but what you continue to get. There's the rub. We are good at assessing the strengths and weaknesses of our colleagues, yet we are demonstrably incompetent when it comes to assessing our own strengths and weaknesses. It is not difficult to understand why: Our egos are *not* invested in rationalizing away other people's shortcomings, but we cannot resist rationalizing our own. Still, only we can change our behavior. To sum up, we can recognize other people's shortcomings, but we cannot change them, and we can remedy our own shortcomings, but we seldom recognize or acknowledge them. This dichotomy is the fundamental "Catch-22" for any attempt to reduce organizational dysfunction. It's the elephant that *never* leaves the room.

We can do better, and *Blueprint* puts us on that path. As we shall see, the collective intelligence of the connected team can overcome pockets of individual Mindset malware. Previously, people outside the team tended to esteem leaders with surface qualities of aggression glossed over with charisma. Meanwhile, the troops inside laid low in their foxholes, fearing friendly fire. Knowing this, we can now turn toward a more conscious form of leadership.

Having established a straightforward and simple pyramid in Chapter 7, rooted in Mindset, the challenge is to purge Mindset malware and ensure that the Mindset Layer is properly aligned and healthy. Ideally, we can imagine being able to build the structure, examine it from all angles, and correct it easily.

TRENDS IN MINDSET DIMENSIONS

In the world of business, awareness and courage have always been coveted Mindset dimensions. Agility seems to have come on the scene with globalization. Markets dominated by monopolies or oligopolies are nearly impossible to maintain in a global market. Also, intuitive-thinking types (i.e., those whose personalities include strengths in intuition and thinking) often dominated leadership. In one company, where the top 20 managers were tested, 19 had this temperament, with only 1 having a sensation-feeling temperament (incidentally, this manager's feelings were hurt when he learned he was the solitary outlier).

Relatedness has emerged more recently as a management principle. Discussions about emotional intelligence, empathy, and collaboration mark this trend. However, the installed base of management mentality probably remains tilted toward thinking-intuition typology, which means that recognizing the need for relatedness itself is problematic. The term "relatedness," suspiciously California-like in its connotations, may engender resistance.

However, the movement is clearly underway. The recent book *Thirteeners: Why Only 13 Percent of Companies Successfully Execute Their Strategy—and How Yours Can Be One of Them* argues that the most successful tier of companies embraces relatedness as an ethic. 13%

down, 87% to go. Now that McKinsey and others have quantified the bottom-line advantage of relatedness, and the advantages to corporate performance become increasingly apparent, we expect the trend will prove to be unstoppable.

CHAPTER 9

DIMENSIONS OF CULTURE AND ENTERPRISE

Understanding the Culture and Enterprise Layers

The dimensions of Culture and Enterprise are dissimilar from those of Mindset, with the latter being more archetypal and therefore more universal, while the former are more of choice. At the Culture Layer, we have:

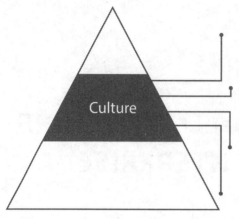

FIGURE 9-1 Four Dimensions of Culture

The four dimensions of the Culture Layer are the attributes we seek most from teams. These dimensions are distinct from the practices discussed in later chapters. These four dimensions of Culture discussed in this section are in turn the desired outputs from practice.

Trust is the glue that holds the team together and strengthens it. The advantages of trust are covered thoroughly in a book I co-authored with Ciancutti, *Built on Trust* (2000).

- **Speed.** Faster resolution, greater agility, shortened cycles
- **Superior intelligence.** Better ideas through access to full knowledge and insight across a team
- **Creativity.** Inspired performance through creative collaboration
- **Self-regulation.** More rapid identification and operational resolution of issues throughout an organization, not just from the top down
- **Capacity.** Ability to address diverse points of view in a heated crucible leading to a new synthesis

- **Meaning.** Being part of something bigger than oneself that is attractive, creative, and productive

In the intervening two decades, a flurry of works has appeared concerning the role of trust in team performance and business outcome. For example, Stephen M.R. Covey in *The SPEED of TRUST: The One Thing That Changes Everything* wrote an entire book about just the first point in the preceding list. Eventually, a neuroscience examination in Paul Zak's *The Neuroscience of Trust* showed that "Compared with people in low-trust companies, people at high-trust companies report: 74% less stress, 106% more energy at work, 50% higher productivity, 13% fewer sick days, 76% more engagement, 29% more satisfaction with their lives, 40% less burnout."

A counterexample concerns The California Department of Transportation ("Caltrans"), a government agency much maligned by drivers in the state. An audit report states, "Caltrans today is significantly out of step with best practice in the transportation field and with the state of California's policy expectations. It is in need of modernization—both in the way it sees its job and how it approaches that job—and *of a culture change that will foster needed adaptation and innovation.*" (Italics added). Its reputation eroded sufficiently enough that an audit was commissioned by The California Department of Transportation. The report was rather scathing, and also identified the paradoxical lack of accountability of the staff, all while they simultaneously feared making decisions. If you are not accountable, why would you be afraid of making decisions? Here is a major leadership challenge: Be decisively accountable. Feel the fear and do it anyway.

Collaboration is the path to creativity and subsequently bottom-line performance. This is the one instance where we use the same term for a dimension and a practice. A culture of collaboration is the outcome we seek, and the practice of collaboration, discussed at length in Chapter 17, is the method for achieving a collaborative outcome.

Coherence is a measure of "togetherness" of the team and includes the critical issue of alignment behind a common vision and purpose.

Incoherence, on the other hand, is a sign of fragmentation, and is what we seek to avoid.

Transparency includes visibility across the organization, which enhances every team member's sense of connection to the whole.

DIMENSIONS OF ENTERPRISE

At the Enterprise Layer, enabled by Culture and by Mindset, teams pursue the four dimensions of Speed, Execution, Innovation, and Customer Intimacy, as illustrated in Figure 9-2.

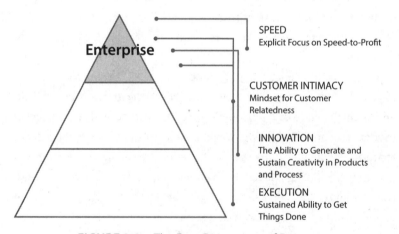

FIGURE 9-2 The Four Dimensions of Enterprise

Notice that we are not using the traditional metrics of business success: revenue, growth, profitability, market cap, and the like. These are the equivalent of looking in the rearview mirror rather than at the road ahead. They rely on the implicit premise that past performance foretells future outcome. Much as this can often provide useful guidance, relying on momentum from past performance can be misleading, especially in a rapidly changing global economy.

SUSTAINING SUCCESS ACROSS THE DIMENSIONS

The dimensions we describe attempt to get closer to the essential ingredients of *sustainable advantage*. Companies that innovate, implement, move quickly, and stay close to customers win. They exemplify strong cultures arising from a healthy mindset in teamwork and leadership.

The main thesis of this book is that understanding the nature of the root causes, the upward migration in the three-layer model, and the importance of hidden factors driving outcome provides a new lens for diagnosing and therefore, to some degree, predicting outcome. What we suggest and prescribe is a new form of "leadership consciousness" as an expanded capability that will be increasingly important in the competitive battleground of tomorrow.

PART III

Foundation Principles

The Why of Leadership

CHAPTER 10

SETTING IT UP

What Teams Want

I f you are planning an effective marketing program, you ask potential customers what features they value, what they want. So, why not invert the traditional question of what management wants from employees and ask instead what *employees* want? What would entice employees to engage fully?

At the outset, we have identified four key factors:

1. Employees want to make a contribution. They come to work wanting to contribute and help move the team forward on its mission. We need a leadership approach that supports that desire and clears the path. By contrast, many organizational leaders harbor, at least unconsciously, what might be called a colonial mentality: Employees are inferiors who need to be controlled, subdued, directed, and continuously monitored. These leaders believe that employees left to their own devices will slack off and cheat at every turn. We have a more positive view of human nature—and see positive results.

2. Employees want to be recognized for their contribution. The root of the word "recognize" means to "see again." The first observation of the contribution is done by the one making it. The second observation, preferably by a broad audience, validates both the action and the actor.

3. Employees want to be seen and heard, not to necessarily win every argument. Behavior that thwarts the opportunity to be seen and heard, such as disrespect, dismissal, or disdain, leaves the potential contributor frustrated in the moment and disinclined to make a similar attempt in the future. Once acknowledged, however, participants experience engagement and can join the flow of the dialogue to a more receptive and productive outcome.

4. Employees want to be part of something bigger than themselves, especially something that reflects and amplifies their inherent values. This transcendent urge is part of human nature. We are, after all, social animals, and from our earliest times we have identified with the broader social group to which we belong.

Addressing what teams want is an essential factor driving the development of *Blueprint*. We can test its ability to deliver what teams want, once the basic framework is in place.

THE MYTHOLOGICAL BASIS
OF COMPLEMENTARITY

As we visit these myths, a few warnings. Having been told and retold through the ages, myths take many forms. Over their lives, they adapt to time and place—but their core lessons endure. We now meet Hermes, the ancient Greek variant of the "trickster," a mythological archetype who appears in different guises worldwide. We start with him, not just for fun or to shake the literal-minded among us, but for reasons that connect with our themes, as you'll see. In time.

· · ·

Hermes was born in a cave on Mount Cyllene in Arcadia in southern Greece. The product of a middle of the night conjugal embrace between philandering Zeus (his wife Hera was off at a women's conference) and Maia (the sleeping daughter of the Titan Atlas), Hermes was just a bit precocious. On his first day of life, he wandered off and found a tortoise, killed it, and used seven strings of sheep gut to shape the tortoise's shell into the first lyre. (Thereby the first lyre was built by the archetypal Liar, as we shall see.)

Skipping his first nap, he then went on to steal 50 cows from his half-brother Apollo. He demonstrated early trickery by fitting the cows with backward false hooves, and wore his sandals backward, to create a track that went in the wrong direction. Or, as some have altered the tale, he taught the cows to walk backward before him, as he erased his own footprints. However he managed it (as a newborn, no less), Hermes was definitely thinking outside the box.

Apollo was *not* amused. He searched far and wide, and finally, based on an anonymous tip, he found his way back to the cave and discovered Hermes. Hermes tried the time-honored trickster defense: Deny everything. He even said he didn't know what a cow was, being only one day old, an "udderly" lame excuse. Unfortunately, he swore his denial on his father's (Zeus's) head. This led Apollo to drag Hermes into an audience with Dad, who was King of the Gods. Zeus *was* amused, and he immediately saw through the fable and forced Hermes to confess and lead Apollo to the herd.

Upon arrival, Apollo noticed two cows had been slaughtered by Hermes in probably the first sacrifice of flesh to the gods. Hermes explained that he had created 12 portions of the meat for the gods. Apollo, math whiz, counted only 11 gods. "Who is the 12th?" he asked. Ever-modest Hermes replied "Me!"

As a gesture of reconciliation, Hermes offered Apollo his lyre. Apollo was enchanted, and offered his herd of cattle in return. Hermes then invented the reed pipe, which he eventually traded for Apollo's golden staff, along with its role of god of herdsmen and shepherds.

In some versions of the myth, Apollo handed the golden shepherd staff over to Hermes not as a trade but as a proof of their friendship. The staff was a short stick entwined by two serpents surmounted by wings; the stick (called the *caduceus*) became Hermes' attribute. In time, the caduceus became a symbol of business and negotiation. Perhaps it was something Apollo and Hermes worked out together, both being gods of shepherds, flocks, and music?

Hermes' pairing with his half-brother, the older Apollo, is not by accident. Thanks to his youth (and pranks), Hermes often embodies aspects of youth, possibility, growth, and unbounded creativity. He needed the influence of someone with experience and stronger boundaries. The moral and rational Apollo was an eagle scout compared to Hermes.

Indeed, theirs was a complementary relationship. In modern terms, you might find Hermes active in the product development meeting room, crossing boundaries, making connections, and thinking outside the box. Apollo possesses the poise and dignity of a CEO. We need the complementary qualities of both Apollo and Hermes in effective leadership teams.

Hermes had an impressive, and often dramatic, career. In Homer's *Iliad*, Hermes used magic to help the King of Troy, Priam, retrieve the body of his dead son, Hector. In the *Odyssey*, Hermes makes three contributions: giving Odysseus an antidote to Circe's magic potion that had turned his men into pigs; convincing Calypso to allow Odysseus to leave the island where he had been kept captive for 10 years; and leading the spirits of the dead killed by Odysseus to the underworld at the end of the story. He recovered Ares, Greek god of war, from the jar that the Aloadai giants had locked him in for almost a year.

Hermes is a force of nature, and his richness as a figure possibly arises from his multitudinous complementary aspects. He is a trickster and a helper. A deceiver and a communicator. He is an inventor (lyre) and the Archetypal Liar, sworn to tell the truth but not the whole truth. The diversity of his character is reflected in his many titles: God of commerce, Patron of thieves and cattle rustlers, Sponsor of gymnasiums and athletics, Overseer of boundaries, Guide to the underworld, Patron of luck. He is a guide for transitions and boundary crossings, protector and benefactor of mortals, magician, sponsor in sports and literature, and, later, the Roman version of the trickster deity, Mercury, inventor of commerce. He was a change agent, prone to action. Courageous, agile, swift, clever, and wily.

•　•　•

The myth of Hermes—of connection and complementarity—has perhaps the most important implications for leadership. This myth has been described as "the central organizing principle of the psyche" and is often referred to as Hermes Duplex, emphasizing his complementary nature. Understanding Hermes is understanding complementarity, which is key to collaboration. In due course, we will see broader applications of the Hermetic trickster myth to business.

So, what do we make of him for leadership? Let's take a first shot at the question. First, Hermes is us. We have all those qualities within us, and although we try to accentuate the positive and deny the negative, we may find the latter emerging under pressure or due to simple lack of self-awareness. He is our raw material in the team, and our task is to regulate his expression.

Think of Hermes as the Connector, not so much a particular person but an ethic. If you want to communicate well in an organization, you need wide paths between one point and another. But paths can be static. The spirit of Hermes can make these paths active. He offers a language and style that enlivens the flow and movement in the system. Hermes connects the rarified atmosphere of the conscious mind and the murky depths of the unconscious. He can penetrate to the deepest layers in the organization to discover hidden problems and concoct creative remedies.

As the god of complementarity, Hermes models the mental agility to switch between modes that we are proposing as an advantage at the team level. Sometimes something clever, wily, or even borderline deceitful is a useful start to a creative process.

Also consider his trickster nature. We all have a trickster side, whether we admit it or not. And often the trickster approach is the first resort considered when facing a new challenge. Whether it is a typically banal exaggeration of marketing claims subsequently refuted by reality, or the more egregious installation of software to create false results for emission testing, trickster behavior is pervasive in organizations. It can be argued that the singular purpose of establishing a high-trust culture, as we promote in this book, is to productively channel or at least constrain the trickster impulse.

The trickster-liar-confession-reconciliation process in the Hermes story of the stolen cows is instructive. The first part—stealing the cows—alienates and fragments, inducing an atmosphere resistant to creativity and collaboration, a common effect of tricksterism. The second part—the gift of the lyre—reintegrates the connection between alienated parties, with the music of the lyre as a compelling symbol for creativity, imagination, and meaning. Hermetic complementarity comes to the fore, the trickster morphs into the reconciler and helper. Hence, the story of Hermes reminds us of the importance of complementarity, and it is relevant to our team and leadership challenges.

He is a change agent, representing a divine call to disruption and transformation being increasingly valuable as once-agile organizations evolve into bureaucracies. Applied properly in contemporary settings, this can have a powerful and useful effect. It can also go badly awry.

Finally, he is immensely entertaining, and there is something about us that is both amused and inspired by a daring rascal figure crossing acceptable boundaries with a sense of abandon.

Hermes (and other mythical characters we will encounter) have both positive and negative aspects, which means, when we understand mythic figures as embodiments of our basic humanity, those same positive and negative aspects appear in our team members, and ourselves. We can anticipate, observe, diagnose, and prepare for the entrance of archetypal behaviors, hopefully minimizing their negative manifestations, while maximizing their positive contributions.

As myths remind us, looking directly into the face of a god (or archetype) can be dangerous. The role of the connected team is to provide a kind of meta-executive function to properly channel Hermes' instigations, subduing the outrageous into the novel and useful.

CHAPTER 11

PRINCIPLES— COMPLEMENTARITY

A Basic Rule of Nature

We now turn to the three basic principles at the bottom layer of the *Blueprint* architecture. First, we consider complementarity's role as a basic "rule of nature" and later relate it to psychology, teamwork, and leadership.

We define complementarity as *two modes of consciousness, mutually exclusive, that cannot be held at the same time but together form a complete pairing.* A simpler definition is understanding that there are always two sides to the matter. While the details of complementarity as a goal in leadership and in teams may seem a bit new, the value of complementarity in nature has been established in multiple instances:

- **Wave–particle duality** in quantum mechanics is probably the most widely recognized example of complementarity in physics. The double-slit experiment, going back to 1801, shows diffraction patterns that are easily explained by light as a wave. On the other hand, the photoelectric effect, which earned the Nobel Prize for Albert Einstein in 1921, describes how electrons are dislodged by light in a manner that can only be explained by viewing light as discrete quantized packets, or particles. The discovery of the photoelectric effect led to the articulation of the theory of wave–particle duality, *the* fundamental paradox underlying quantum mechanics.

- The secret of **DNA** was unraveled using the principle of complementarity. This happened slowly though, because nearly 100 years passed between Swiss chemist Friedrich Miescher's original discovery of DNA in the 1860s and the double-helix breakthrough by British molecular biologist Francis Crick and American molecular biologist James Watson in 1953. As in the case of wave–particle duality, the solution was forced upon our cultural consciousness through evolving experimentation and discovery.

- **Matter and anti-matter.** In 1928, British physicist Paul Dirac published his wave equation that demonstrated the theoretical possibility of anti-matter as a mirror image of matter. Shortly thereafter, the existence of the anti-electron (the positron) was demonstrated in the laboratory. Theory has it that matter and anti-matter were created in the Big Bang, although the low quantity of currently observed anti-matter compared to matter (the "Baryon Asymmetry") is considered to be one of the great unsolved problems in physics. Nonetheless, the complementarity principle in matter/anti-matter has been firmly established.

- **Electricity and magnetism** were considered opposites until 1865 when James Clerk Maxwell, a Scottish physicist and mathematician, integrated them through his elegant equations. The term "electromagnetic" reflects their integration into one underlying phenomenon despite their strikingly different manifestations in nature.

The notion of complementarity as a solution to paradoxical physical phenomena was arrived at only after attempts to explain nature free of such paradoxes ("Linear Thinking") failed and overwhelming evidence for complementarity emerged from scientific observations and experiments. Given the ubiquity of the need for complementary thinking, we might refer to this as the Law of Complementarity. Even today, some scientists regard complementarity with distaste, almost as a concession to the defeat of linear thinking with regard to certain fundamental natural phenomena. In attempts to apply complementarity to psychology, teamwork and leadership encounter similar resistance from linear thinkers in the domain of business.

Complementarity is like trying to see both sides of a coin at the same time. Difficult, yet obviously the existence of two sides is inherent in the nature of the coin itself. Getting your head around complementarity *is* difficult, and no wonder we prefer more simplistic, one-sided explanations for the world around us. Yet complementarity provides substantial benefits to teamwork, and part of the leadership task is to overcome resistance to it. Fortunately, the movement to complementarity also provides relief from defending often-indefensible black-and-white positions and is frequently accompanied by a sense of liberation from dogmatism.

So, how do we get from complementarity as a basic rule of nature to a basic reality in leadership? Well, theories of mind already reference multiple versions of complementarity, including conscious/unconscious, right brain/left brain, intellectual/emotional, sensing/intuitive, and masculine/feminine. Let's see how they apply to leadership.

COMPLEMENTARY TWINNING

We define "twinning" as a mode of unconditional partnering of two people committed to a common goal. Twinning has long been around in business as a *de facto*, real phenomenon. There are simply too many instances of twinning in business not to hypothesize that some natural, hidden forces are at work. These twinning examples are not necessarily friends nor arranged marriages. They are simply cases of two people getting together and achieving results far beyond what might have been possible as solo leaders. A few prominent Silicon Valley examples: Robert Noyce and Gordon Moore of Intel, and then their successors Andy Grove and Craig Barrett, about which many accounts have been written; Larry Page and Sergey Brin of Google; Bill Hewlett and David Packard of Hewlett-Packard.

Recently, Rich Karlgaard and Michael Malone in *Team Genius: The New Science of High-Performing Organizations*, investigated the prevalence of twinning, what they call "partnering," in business. With impressive research, they assembled a vast collection of types of partnering. They conclude that twinning can produce astonishing results. Two examples: Apple, where Steve Jobs produced his famous innovations only when accompanied by a partner (and was comparatively fallow without) and Alcoholics Anonymous, which simply might not have existed without the unlikely chance encounter and subsequent twinning of Bill Wilson and Bob Smith (a.k.a., Bill W. and Dr. Bob), a stockbroker and surgeon. It is as if twinning can create amazing results not otherwise possible, seemingly *ex nihilo*, out of nothing.

We actually see three types of partnering. Merging involves the breakdown of interpersonal boundaries, usually in a pathological manner. For example, codependency—a dysfunctional helping relationship where one person supports or enables another person's drug addiction, alcoholism, gambling addiction, poor mental health, immaturity, irresponsibility, or underachievement. A second is Mirroring, which involves the ability to reflect one another's feelings and perspectives but without unconditional commitment. The third is Twinning, a state of unconditional commitment grounded in complementarity.

Consistent with the theme of this book, we aim to dig deeper into the twinning phenomenon and understand the underlying forces that initiate and sustain twinning. Twinning has a certain natural pull. Examining it further, we see that understanding the twinning phenomenon and learning to practice twinning can benefit both leaders and organizations for the long haul.

In particular, and consistent with the themes in this book, we think the best mode of twinning involves complementarity in both skills and outlook. This might include external/internal, technology/business, extravert/introvert, strategic/tactical, financial/operational, logical/psychological, and any other complementary possibilities. Complementarity seems to be the way that nature frames certain kinds of creativity, manifested into decisions and action by twinning. An even stronger version of twinning involves certain underlying archetypal dimensions, which will be described shortly.

For some people, the benefits of twinning are hard to see. Our cultural predisposition to old leadership thinking often dominates, blinding us to a different mode of interaction.

Yet it can't be denied that twinning has immense power, and its absence is probably a major cause of failure. Either/or thinking leads to fragmentation, narcissism, power-tripping, cost, and lost time. By contrast, twinning induces a state of mind receptive to complementarity that is the antidote for either/or thinking.

As psychologist and author Daniel Goleman points out in "Social Intelligence and the Biology of Leadership": "the leader–follower dynamic is not a case of two (or more) independent brains reacting consciously or unconsciously to each other. Rather, the individual minds become in a sense fused into a single system. We believe that great leaders are those whose behavior powerfully leverages the system of brain interconnectedness."

Twinning is applied empathy, where participants accept the rule that one must go first and not wait for the other to yield ground. The result is increased connection and trust in a relationship where ideas flourish and creativity makes its welcome contribution.

TWINNING: RESISTANCE AND BENEFITS

The discussion of twinning would not be complete without acknowledging possible resistance to its adoption. One reaction is to the term "twinning" itself. Some find it too squishy. We prefer it. However, using "partnering" as an alternative term may facilitate acceptance.

A second source of resistance is more problematic. We will shortly describe the Solo Hero archetype and the common phenomenon of solar addiction. Some simply cannot countenance giving up the (often illusory) full autonomy of these conditions, and relinquishing power to a partnership. There is also the fear of appearing "weak" to share power. In one instance, the CEO of a relatively small public company had a much more experienced board member who repeatedly offered to take a more active role in the company from his board position. The CEO had strong skills in public markets, M&A, and financing, yet was a poor operations manager. The board member had strong credentials in marketing and operations management. A potential complementarity. However, the CEO consistently refused the offer of help. Meanwhile, performance deteriorated, and the stock price declined *99.98%* from its prior high at the time of this writing, with nearly 100 million dollars in accumulated deficit.

Once resistance is surmounted, twinning can provide the following outsized benefits to leadership:

- **Performance.** Cases as diverse as Apple Computer and Alcoholics Anonymous illustrate how the serendipitous formation of twinning partnerships have created world-famous, and world-changing, outcomes. Twinning may also be considered a form of "power mentoring," and an advance on well-established mentoring programs broadly employed today.
- **Execution.** The demanding dual tasks of conceiving breakthrough business and product concepts, along with instilling high-performance teamwork, may be more readily achieved when talented people combine different perspectives and capabilities.
- **Creativity.** The combined intellectual and intuitive capacities of twins operating in unconditional collaboration easily outpace the capability of solo leadership.

- **Meaning.** The experience of creating unexpected and outsized results creates a powerful sense of purpose in the team, validating their contribution and inspiring further contributions.

All of this adds up to creating an enduring competitive advantage. The organization doesn't just become a platform for a particular business program, but a generator of creative programs into the future. Its performance advantage radiates outward to its customers, forging enduring links. Hewlett-Packard created a culture that provided a sustained advantage which lasted decades.

Howard and I have been able to implement an approach to improving leadership and teamwork that neither of us could have developed on our own. Twinning helps defeat organizational dysfunctionality. To understand that challenge, we will shortly take another look at that darker side of team life, from both a mythic and contemporary point of view.

CHAPTER 12

COMPLEMENTARITY
IN LEADERSHIP

Business books abound with theories and recommendations about organizational structures and methods, often advocating one in particular. If businesses and people were truly one size fits all, that might work. But businesses, teams, and employees need plans that suit their circumstances. The potential applications for complementarity in business are virtually endless. Our purpose is to introduce the concept, so you can see how it works. To get that process started, let's address some concrete examples of complementarity.

TWO BASIC AXES OF COMPLEMENTARITY

We have already seen one instance of complementarity in leadership: the progression of mindset in product development. As organizations go through the process of developing a "product"—whether a physical product, a software package, or a service offering—they encounter a need for two different modes of consciousness. Initially, in what we might call the Creative Mode, the emphasis is on fluidity, inventiveness, and access to the deep imagination. Leadership needs to support this process by nurturing the opportunity for creative collaboration. Over time, as design concepts become solidified, the leadership challenge shifts to what might be called the Execution Mode, with its focus on schedules, budget, and coordination across multiple functions in service of an overall launch plan. This continuous shift from the creative mode to the execution mode is illustrated in Figure 12-1. The conscious leader needs to be aware of the need for transition between these two modes and manage the team's expectations and outlook along the way.

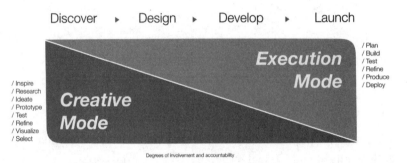

FIGURE 12-1 Two Complementary Modes in "Product" Development

Along a different dimension, another basic complementary pairing has to do with what we might call Open/Collaborative and Directive/Demanding Modes. At one end of this spectrum, there is a need to encourage an open and collaborative culture in line with the mandates of this book. At the other end, there is sometimes the need for clear direction. In the *Harvard Business Review* classic "Demand Better Results—And Get Them," author Robert Schaffer argues that having all the systems in place is by itself not adequate for execution. Instead, sometimes the leader needs to put a stake in the ground and demand results from the team. This suggests another dynamic interaction between two modes of consciousness.

The interplay between these two complementary pairs is illustrated in Figure 12-2. This places requirements on the leadership to recognize these alternative modes in the first place, and then determine the "operating point" in this diagram at any one time, depending on the current circumstances. This is not an argument for balance, but rather for dynamic adjustment over time, although the more frequent state will be toward the center of the diagram as illustrated.

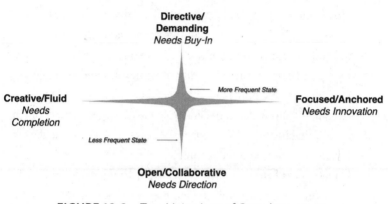

FIGURE 12-2 Two Major Axes of Complementarity

There are some other immediately obvious instances of complementarity in business, such as the following.

- **Cooperation versus Competition.** The (often unappealing) term *co-opetition* has been coined as a way to describe the concept of cooperative competition. In *The M-Form Society*, Ouchi famously described this form of interaction as "an unnatural act." That characterization gets us closer to the acceptance of paradox that is necessary to work with complementarity.
- **Strategy versus Objectives.** Fierce debates rage around whether to plan with a focus on strategy (means) or on objectives (ends). A complete picture requires both objectives and strategy—so flip a coin and get underway. A company may declare: "We aim to be the leading provider of . . ." but without more—without the how—what happens? Show us the strategy to get to that position, and the devil—lying in the details—will

inform of us as to its impracticality. In that instance, strategy reforms objectives and cures its inflation.

- **Content versus Process Focus.** Conscious managers seek out the challenge of complementarity thinking. Leaders have to manage two aspects of their roles. One deals with the content of the business, including strategy, market conditions, competitor moves, and financial status. The other is the state of the system, including the quality of internal communication and teamwork, accountability against commitments, creativity, degree of trust, and the panoply of principles and practices described in this book. A leader needs to be able to switch focus back and forth between these two areas, at times continuously. Placing all of one's attention on only one is like standing on one leg. Eventually things get wobbly.
- **Team versus One-on-One Meetings.** There is no need to justify team meetings. One-on-one meetings obviously allow for topics such as personal development, feedback on performance, and compensation matters. Also, when teams are not yet fully acclimated to the idea of open communication supported by diplomatic immunity in the staff meeting, a team member can bring up sensitive issues in a one-on-one meeting as a test. This allows the leader to encourage open communication and help team members move through the inevitable process of getting comfortable with that mode of team communication, especially where that mode differs from prior leadership.

David Whyte in *The Heart Aroused: Poetry and the Preservation of the Soul in Corporate America* talks about the process of finding our voice this way:

The voice carries the emotional body of the person speaking. The voice is as important to our identity as anything we possess. We ask ourselves if we really have a voice in this organization, want reassurance that we can give voice to our opinions, and if we cannot, speak *sotto voce* to those few in whom we choose to confide.

The problem, Whyte avers, is that "In our first attempts at courageous speech, in the meeting room or empty page, we prepare to roar like a lion and deliver, instead, the timorous speech of a mouse." Accepting our mouse voice is the beginning of moving toward more lion-like speech. And the humbling realization of our starting point as a mouse reminds us of the virtues of compassion for the other side when roaring like a lion later.

Staff meetings are the stage on which the physical configuration of the team and the emotional/intuitive team coincide. This is an important conjunction for the development of the connected team. Ideally, the team, now proficient in practices and competent in creative tension without dogmatism, enjoys the additional reinforcement of a direct visual and aural sensory experience. In this context, creative teamwork can flourish. In addition, offsites provide an opportunity for the team to move into a *peer relationship*, breaking down barriers associated with reporting lines of authority.

- **Top-Down versus Bottom-Up Planning.** Top-down planning is often simpler and faster because there are fewer variables and simpler calculations. Yet this type of planning can be laden with hidden idealized fantasies. Unless uncovered and examined early on, the prospects for meeting expectations are slim. Bottom-up planning can get lost in the weeds. We have seen bottom-up resource forecasts that exceeded likely requirements by over 400%. The cure is an iterative top-down, bottom-up process (wave-particle, wave-particle...) that defends against the potential downsides of either method alone. Complementarity in action.
- **Strategic versus Tactical.** What is the difference between strategic and tactical? Confusion or lack of clarity about these terms results in meandering discussions that lead nowhere.

One problem is a lack of clear boundaries in the very definitions of the terms. Strategic means "consequential," "determinative," "all-important," and "crucial." Tactical means "appropriate," "expedient" and "sound." Sometimes the distinctions are difficult to parse, but the experienced eye knows the difference. Explicitly recognizing when the team is in one mode or the other, and iterating back and forth between them, helps avoid either/or thinking that inflates the importance of one mode at the expense of the other. The iterative interaction between strategy and tactics brings more possibilities to the forefront.

In one company, the VP of Sales, when asked his strategy to penetrate a market segment adjacent to an existing segment, replied that his "strategy" was to change the commission plan for his sales force. That's a tactic, not a strategy. Strategic considerations in this context might include market demographics, customer pain points the product could remedy, the availability of key partners, and pricing and discount strategy.

Seeking complementarity requires more effort than either/or thinking. Either/or is simpler: Pick a position and hold your ground. Avoid ambiguity. But life is full of ambiguity. All aspects of leadership, and as we have seen, in nature, demand a more sophisticated perspective, one that can grapple with apparently contradictory elements of reality. Complementarity adds that dimension. When you are willing to pay the price to acquire a deeper perceptual apparatus, you are rewarded by moving closer to reality and improving your odds of better outcomes.

CHAPTER 13

GOING DEEPER

Complementary Archetypes: Solar/Lunar

As Howard Teich explains, light itself has been associated with human awareness for thousands of years. There are two sources of light: the sun and the moon. Solar light represents a direct mode; lunar, a reflective mode. Makes sense, right? Solar is direct light from the sun; lunar light is reflected light. We can then translate that distinction into an *internal mode of human thinking*. The reflective, lunar mode of consciousness generates a possibility that is then transferred to the solar mode for action. In that sense, lunar has a powerful (and too often underrated) role in human behavior. To summarize, lunar thinking is intuitive, insight-focused, and non-linear. It provides the context for action. Solar thinking is rational, action-focused, and linear. It acts on the world.

To be effective, these two modes must collaborate. Simply put, lunar awareness without action is passive. Solar action ungrounded in some purposeful context derived from the lunar can lead to purposeless, erratic, or even destructive outcomes. Here, we explore the need for solar/lunar balance, its contributions to creative collaboration, and identify the consequences of imbalance between the two modes.

For centuries, cultures have placed solar in a dominant position over lunar. Early civilization placed an important priority on survival and being able to outwit, outmaneuver, and physically overwhelm one's enemies. Dominance prevailed over relationships, and leaders were rewarded for being strong and aggressive. Lunar qualities of emotional intelligence and awareness were discounted. In today's search for competitive advantage, however, leadership needs not so much to dominate as to guide and inspire, and lunar's importance is on the rise. We have seen many cases of "solar addiction," where a leader refuses to step outside the dimensions of linear thinking.

Identifying solar with traditionally masculine qualities, and lunar with traditionally feminine qualities, is a big mistake. Joint solar/ lunar consciousness demands more of us. In *Solar Light Lunar Light*, Howard Teich insists, "each gender has both solar and lunar attributes." He encourages us to consider how "we might free humanity from the double bind of that binary which denies men…a right to access their lunar sides, and women…any access to solar ascendancy in the world." What he describes does not fall into the pattern of men are from Mars, women are from Venus; it does not divide consciousness into two, rather it recognizes that both exist in each of us. As he puts it, "All of us possess both solar and lunar capacities. To be both logical and intuitive as well as strong and caring is a natural state of being. We have all inherited these age-old capabilities."

There's a lot to ponder here. As with complementarity, this is not a linear explanation; it's not either/or. It's both. In fact, Howard specifically warns not to confuse complementary patterns with "Western culture's way of splitting pairs into conflicting opposites." Depending upon your background, resisting that inclination may take some mental adjustment. To understand better solar/lunar qualities, Teich's Solar/ Lunar Assessment chart can be quite useful. It can be found here: solarlunar.com/articles/quick-fix/solar-lunar-assessment-chart/.

For example, a colleague who was a specialist in implementing time-based product development excitedly declared one day that he had realized that a "conflict of the opposites"—a buttoned-down product-development program versus being able to turn on a dime—was at the heart of his approach to reducing cycle time in product development. His insight was off the mark. The competitive advantage he sought requires both an ability to focus relentlessly on the task at hand and a parallel ability to know when to drop everything and move forward along a different path. His mistake was defining a *conflict* between two modes of operation which reflects the dominant reductionist mindset prevalent in leadership thinking. The more accurate diagnosis is complementarity: Different circumstances require a different mindset.

A main thesis of this book is that establishing and maintaining solar/lunar balance can lead to a leap in creativity and engagement—qualities that are essential for success. Making the transition to a balanced solar/lunar mindset requires serious effort. It requires a willingness to add new perspectives, which are often hard to reconcile with established habits of thought. If certain quarters refuse the calling to a higher level of functioning, what happens? Possibly, over time, the advantage of this method will become increasingly apparent, leading to its preferred adoption and improved competitive advantage.

FROM SOLO HERO TO COMPLEMENTARY HEROES

Here, we address the myth of the Solo Hero and its limitations for leadership. This may cause confusion with the example of Han Solo, a widely admired hero figure from Star Wars. Han Solo, in fact, was a rogue and on his own in the early part of the story, but eventually changes his mind to join with the rebel team to a successful ending. So, his actions meant he transitioned from a solo hero to a leader who inspired a highly functional team to achieve its mission. While using the term "Lone Hero" may steer us away from thinking of the Han Solo figure, we will continue with "Solo Hero" given its more frequent use in our context.

Solo Heroes

Solo Hero myths hold many lessons—both positive and negative—for teamwork and leadership. Our central story of the solo hero is the Greek hero Hercules, the offspring of Zeus and a (married) mortal. When Hera, Zeus's jealous wife, found out, she was enraged and determined to kill Hercules in revenge. Her first attempt, when Hercules was a newborn, failed. For her second attempt, Hera struck the adult Hercules with a fit of madness, during which he killed his wife and children. Upon his recovery, Hercules, full of remorse, was directed by an oracle to repent by going to King Eurystheus of Tiryns and doing what the king commanded. What followed was the famous Twelve Labors of Hercules.

Despite being the son of the King of the Gods, which accounted for his enormous strength, Hercules was mortal, impulsive, and amazingly thin-skinned. He threatened to shoot the sun ("sometime too hot the eye of heaven shines") and to beat up the ocean. After completing the Twelve Labors, he had an opportunity to quietly retire and remarry. Instead, driven by his lack of restraint and impulsive nature, he went off on adventures that eventually led to his doom. Hercules was consumed by power and left devastation along his journey through life. Could he have led a team?

The qualities of the solo hero may be appropriate to leading a group in some circumstances. But movements based on solo heroes who require adoration and obedience from followers often turn out badly. Think of the Jonestown mass suicide. In November 1978, 900 Americans died from self-administered cyanide poisoning under the spell (or command) of Jim Jones, the leader of the People's Temple religious organization. Granted, this is a notorious case, but one needn't look far to find other movements and organizations that have suffered under the sway of solo heroes.

Does this mean that solo heroes cannot found and lead companies? Absolutely not. Due to luck, timing, or extraordinary talent, companies can pull off the most amazing results under the most eccentric leadership. Tempting though it may be to consider Steve Jobs as a leading example of a successful solo hero leader, Rich Karlgaard and Michael Malone point out in *Team Genius* that Jobs produced amazing results only when he was paired with a complementary twin. They introduce the notion of organizational twinning and reinforce skepticism about the solo hero approach. All too often, a solo hero refuses advice and assistance offered by potential helpers he encounters along his journey who might balance his lopsided consciousness.

From Solo Hero to Complementary Twinning

Consider this: Hercules, for all his bluster and strength, would have failed in his labors had he not made good use of advice from the goddess Athena. The thought bears repeating: Hercules, a solo hero if ever there was one, needed and accepted advice and help. From his half-sister, no less.

Athena exhibited a broad spectrum of positive qualities. She was said to represent intelligence, humility, consciousness, cosmic knowledge, creativity, education, enlightenment, the arts, and eloquence in power. Basically, truth, justice, and moral values. While she and her brother Ares were both deities of war, their styles were a study in contrasts. Ares was inclined to slaughter and bloodshed. Even-tempered Athena was known to favor wisdom over violence to resolve conflicts; she was extraordinarily courageous and never lost a battle. It is no surprise, then, that she was also closely associated with Nike, the goddess of victory.

Athena was active in helping out many mythological figures. In his first labor, Hercules faced the terrifying Nemean Lion. This beast had an impenetrable hide, and Hercules was only able to kill it by strangulation. But the task required that he skin it, and so he was stumped. Athena's help in showing how to use one of the lion's claws to skin the strangled beast enabled Hercules to complete the first of his tasks. (Despite his image as a solo hero, Hercules, on several occasions, relied on her help to successfully complete the remainder of the Twelve Labors.)

How then, we might wonder, has Hercules wound up being billed as a prime example of the solo hero? Might it be that over time, the more collaborative parts of the story were glossed over in the retelling, perhaps in an attempt to make Hercules seem more heroic? Is there something that calls us as mere mortals to want to enhance the glory of a mythical solo hero? Or is there another perspective we might consider?

In their 2013 book *The Athena Doctrine: How Women (and the Men Who Think Like Them) Will Rule the Future*, John Gerzema and Michael D'Antonio attempt to derive modern wisdom from the Athena myth. They argue that the world would be a better place if values and habits they categorize as feminine replaced the typical masculine, dominating style. They are supported by extensive research, in which they found that "nearly two-thirds of people around the world—including the majority of men—feel that the world would be a better place if men thought more like women ... regardless of age, income, or nation."

Their use of feminine/masculine as a behavioral discriminator poses problems, however. First, it's rife with irrelevant associations and improper connotations. It is too simplistic automatically to conflate "feminine" with "women." Two of the traits strongly related to leadership that are considered masculine are "aggressive" and "decisive." If that's the case, then would "passive" and "indecisive" be feminine? Such categorizations come across as affronts to women. Similarly, one of the traits strongly related to leadership that the authors categorize as feminine is "reasonable." It would not be unreasonable for men to take umbrage at that. If "flexible" is feminine, does that imply that "inflexible" is masculine? And what about the trait of "plans for the future," which falls in the feminine category? Does that mean the masculine ethic does not "plan for the future"?

The authors may have measured something other than what they assumed, namely the stereotypical association of qualities with gender, a dubious assumption. At one point during the 1980s, I managed an organization with eight women who seemed to believe the path to success was to act like men (or adopt the masculine traits described in Athena). They were aggressive, oppositional, critical, and could not coalesce into a real team, just like many male teams I have observed. In my experience, the narrative path of *The Athena Doctrine* goes off on a tangent and is neither useful nor accurate.

Yes, there is duality implicit in the terms feminine and masculine. But I prefer to analyze issues of teamwork and leadership in terms of solar/lunar complementarity and acknowledge that these traits are gender-neutral and disassociated from gender. The solar/lunar discriminant can shed more light on the topic and sidestep the pitfalls of typecasting either masculine or feminine.

If we look more deeply into the "feminine" qualities described in *The Athena Doctrine*, we see abilities and traits that are very similar to the themes of this book: communication, empathy, collaboration, and avoidance of either/or thinking. Without sorting traits into masculine or feminine, we can see that Athena demonstrated a rare case of balance, in contrast to her mythological colleagues. Ares was all about combat, Hercules about brute strength, and Zeus about serial recreational procreation. By contrast, Athena showed great courage, never backed down from a dangerous encounter, yet demonstrated compassion and fairness in her dealings. A mediator, diplomat, and advisor, as well as a warrior and a thinker, she was considered the wisest of the Greek gods and goddesses—and her many remarkable exploits validate Athena's demonstrated balance of solar/lunar qualities.

Given her courage, initiative, fairness, logic, reasoning, consciousness, and creativity, she was one of the most important figures in Greek mythology. Known primarily as the goddess of wisdom, she was famous for her more solar traits of strength, courage, sense of justice, strategy in war, and mathematics. She also was known as the goddess of crafts, and seen as the patron goddess of musicians, painters, sculptors, weavers, and other arts, which involve lunar traits.

Athena is a strong and just feminine figure, a model for women today. She is the embodiment of positive solar/lunar qualities operating in balance, something to which all of us can aspire.

CONTEMPORARY REFUTATION
OF THE SOLO HERO MYTH

Joshua Wolf Shenk has written a critique and refutation of the solo hero myth called *Powers of Two: Finding the Essence of Innovation in Creative Pairs*. He examines the partnership of Paul McCartney and John Lennon in the Beatles. He notes that McCartney and Lennon could not be more different: meticulous versus sloppy, diplomatic versus provocative, patient versus impatient, thin-skinned versus thick-skinned. Yet they produced great music together.

While some credit the Beatles' accomplishments to individual contributions, Shenk disagrees:

> For centuries, the myth of the lone genius has towered over us, its shadow obscuring the way creative work really gets done. The attempts to pick apart the Lennon-McCartney partnership reveal just how misleading that myth can be, because John and Paul were so obviously more creative as a pair than as individuals, even if at times they appeared to work in opposition to each other. The lone-genius myth prevents us from grappling with a series of paradoxes about creative pairs: that distance doesn't impede intimacy, and is often a crucial ingredient of it; that competition and collaboration are often entwined. … If that seems far-fetched, it's because our cultural obsession with the individual has obscured the power of the creative pair.
>
> The accidental encounter of these two geniuses, so different and yet so productive despite their competitive natures, suggests potential that can be tapped by proactively forming partnerships using the collaborative techniques we have outlined here.

In a working paper on leadership, *Leadership Excellence and the "Soft" Skills*, David Bradford and Carole Robin declare, "In fact, the institution that is dependent on the solo brilliant leader is in a very vulnerable, unsustainable position."

CHAPTER 14

MORE GOING DEEPER

Complementary Archetypes: Puer/Senex

Another complementarity archetype essential to leadership is seen in *puer* and *senex*. Latin for "eternal boy," puer is the root of the word "puerile" meaning "childishly foolish." Puer contains aspects of youth, possibility, growth, and unbounded creativity. By contrast, senex, meaning "old man," contains the complementary aspects of age, discipline, order, and responsibility. Puer and senex constitute a nearly co-dependent pair, in which excessive puer constellates the need for senex, and overbearing senex withers without a puer influence.

Admittedly, concepts like puer and senex do not typically arise in business conversations. So why discuss them here? Our purpose is to show how to identify puer and senex in the organization. With that knowledge, you can then seek a balance between them that will improve team performance.

PUER

As with any mythological archetype, puer shows up in many elaborate forms down through the centuries. Perhaps you're already thinking of young Icarus falling from the sky. Or James Barrie's Peter Pan flying about in Neverland. Pop psychology has described the "Peter Pan Syndrome" in men as those who won't grow up. More recently, Michael Jackson was a contemporary puer figure with his replication of Peter Pan's world in his Californian Neverland Ranch.

Puer also shows up in the world of business in several guises, and you'll see more than a few examples of this throughout the book. Often, investors are inclined to place a high premium on an entrepreneur's "passion." Perhaps what really is important is *directed passion*, passion informed by competence, realism, and practicality. Watch out for the seductive appeal of a charismatic puer, especially in the high-tech industry, where inflation and hubris often run rampant.

SENEX

Senex is associated with the Roman god Saturn, a derivative of the earlier Greek figure Cronus, who was the earliest senex figure in the Western tradition. A descendent of the original gods Uranus (the sky) and Gaia (the earth), Cronus came to power as a ruling Titan by castrating his Father Uranus. Not surprisingly, given what he had done, Cronus was extremely worried about the future power of his children. To secure his dominion, he ate them! His wife Rhea managed to rescue one son, Zeus, by hiding him in the Dictean Cave in Crete. She then gave Cronus a stone wrapped in the clothes of the infant; Cronus promptly swallowed the stone. Thus, Rhea succeeded in making Cronus believe he had killed all his children. When Zeus reached maturity, he overpowered and dethroned his father and made Cronus disgorge his siblings. (How's that for putting family dinners in a different light?)

A mellower version of senex appears in the Wise Old Man arche-type, such as Obi-Wan Kenobi throughout most of the Star Wars saga, Maz (the Wise Old Woman) in the 2015 movie (Star Wars: The Force Awakens), and sages, wizards, mentors, hermits, and dwarfs throughout storytelling. Senex embodies the qualities of responsibil-ity, order, focus, limitation, boundaries, and personal responsibility—the attitude of "the buck stops here."

Senex plays a critical role in leadership, grounding and executing puer's imaginative flights of fancy. Senex also has a negative aspect. Excessive senex displays rigidity, cynicism, and acidity. Hillman says "We shall never encounter the good wise old man without recogniz-ing him as an ogre at the same time" (as cited by Margot McLean in *Senex and Puer: Uniform Edition of the Writings of James Hillman*).

The complementarity of solar/lunar and puer/senex leads to the notion of two people joining forces, where each person in the pair embodies one side of the complementarity. This gives rise to solar/lunar or puer/senex twinning. As we have seen, Hermes and Apollo held opposite sides of the puer/senex complementarity. This notion of twinning provides a powerful basis for partnering and can lead to extraordinary results.

DAEDALUS AND ICARUS/HELIOS AND PHAETON

The Mythic Basis for Puer/Senex

Previous chapters highlighted a jumble of hidden issues through which we must navigate to reach the root causes of organizational behavior. These issues are often deeply hidden and are rarely identified or discussed. Yet for businesses to succeed, we have to recognize their existence. We need to see through them, get past the barriers, adapt, and develop solutions. As we learn to navigate the Culture and Mindset layers, let's illustrate some of the relevant issues with the story of Daedalus and Icarus.

. . .

In Greek mythology, Daedalus and Icarus, father and son, find themselves locked in a tower within the Labyrinth with no release date. To set the stage for their predicament, we need to introduce King Minos of Crete, yet another of Zeus's sons by mortal women. Think of Minos as a typical, egocentric, manipulative, hierarchical figure, a predecessor of the type of CEO, insistent on top-down hierarchies with deferential staff that we want to supplant.

When the former king died, Minos declared himself to be king. But by what authority? Well, he simply asserted that he was approved for the office by the gods. (In today's world, he'd have wrangled and announced approval from the board of directors.)

Next, to demonstrate proof of the gods' approval, Minos asked the god Poseidon to send an offering suitable for his ascension to the throne. Lo and behold, Poseidon sent a magnificent bull to sacrifice to the god. Instead, Minos succumbed to a colossal case of hubris and kept the bull, to improve the breeding quality of his cattle.

Poseidon was furious. In retaliation, he arranged for Minos's wife Pasiphae to fall in love with the bull. Skipping over the salacious details of the affair, the bull impregnated Pasiphae, who gave birth to the Minotaur: half man, half bull.

Now, where to keep this beast? The ingenious Daedalus, an architect who had been exiled from Athens, created the Labyrinth, a structure so complex that even Daedalus himself needed to reference the original blueprints to find his way out. (This is not an uncommon outcome in today's software startups.) The Minotaur settled into his new home. But there was trouble ahead.

The Minotaur ate humans. His meals included seven boys and seven girls sent from Athens as tribute after losing a war with Crete. The Greek hero Theseus had himself included in the group, intending to set things right and kill the Minotaur. Theseus used a ball of string (courtesy of Daedalus) to trace his route into the Labyrinth, kill the Minotaur, and find his way out again. He then rescued the sacrificial youths and returned them to Athens.

Minos was furious. Knowing that only Daedalus was clever enough to have provided a way out of the Labyrinth, he incarcerated Daedalus and his son Icarus in the Labyrinth, vowing never to release them.

Daedalus constructed two pairs of wings so he and Icarus could fly out of the Labyrinth. He warned Icarus in advance not to fly too close to the sun—lest the wax melt and the wings come unstuck—and not to fly too close to the sea—lest the humidity unseal the feathers from the wax. Icarus dutifully agreed. But once airborne he got carried away. Icarus flew as high as he could. As his father had warned, the sun melted the wax holding his wings together, and Icarus plunged to his death in the sea while Daedalus watched in horror.

A classic puer figure, Icarus ignores the sensible advice of his father, a classic senex figure. He succumbs instead to his puer impulsiveness. The fate of Icarus demonstrates the potentially dire consequences of straying too far from the psychological balance of puer-senex complementarity.

If its prevalence in mythology is a clue, the puer-senex mindset is a prominent factor in human behavior. Another story with similar themes is of Phaeton, as told by Ovid in his *Metamorphoses*. Phaeton brags to his buddies that he is the son of Helios, god of the sun. When they refuse to believe him, he gets his mom to set up a meeting with his father, whom he asks, presumptuously, to prove that he is indeed his father. Helios falls for the ploy and promises to grant him any wish. So, Phaeton asks to be allowed to drive the chariot of the sun for an entire day. But keeping the chariot on course from early morning to sunset is a tricky matter, and Helios, consulting his senex nature, is appropriately worried. Messing with the course of the sun could have devastating consequences. Unfortunately, Helios eventually accedes to his son's request.

Disaster ensues. Phaeton drives the divine horses too close to the earth, scorching crops and animals and drying up lakes and rivers. This time it is Zeus, the ultimate Chairman of the Board, who strikes Phaeton with lightning, thus turning him into the constellation The Charioteer, an abrupt ending to a very brief career.

The fact that there are two stories sharing a curious and instructive theme may indicate that the ancients harbored a significant fear about hubris. Daedalus is a highly intelligent and gifted inventor, yet he evidently could not foretell that hubris would drive Icarus to disobey his counsel. Otherwise, he might have tethered Icarus to his own flight, thus maintaining control and protecting his son. Likewise, Helios was smart and strong. As Chief Solar Officer, he had to be in order to manage the course of the sun through the heavens every day. Yet he was blind to the obvious likelihood of Phaeton's mismanagement. Perhaps if they had gone along on each journey as coaches—Daedalus guiding Icarus, and Helios beside Phaeton in the Chariot—the adventures would not have ended in tragedy.

The story of Daedalus and Icarus presents a complementary pair, each with its upside and downside attributes. The prevalence of this and other puer/senex stories (e.g., Helios and Phaeton) indicate a common occurrence of puer/senex conflict. Each of these stories usually results in a catastrophe, so we can infer that mythology warns us that puer/senex imbalance can be hazardous.

CHAPTER 15

PRINCIPLES—EMPATHY

The Master Emotion

W e now describe the principle of empathy first because it pervasively affects the practices and skills we advocate. Considered "the master emotion," empathy is a prerequisite for building an engaged team. Developing, building, and maintaining teamwork demands deep, trusting interaction, for which empathy is an absolute requirement. Empathy is also vital for the psychological safety of all concerned.

NEUROSCIENCE OF EMPATHY

The neurological basis for empathy has been revealed by the accidental discovery of mirror neurons. Italian researchers in the 1990s were working with macaque monkeys when the same pattern of neuron firing was observed in both an action and the observation of an action. They found that some macaque neurons would respond in the same way when the monkey saw a person pick up a piece of food, as when the monkey picked up the food itself. Subsequent expanded studies have confirmed the existence of mirroring properties in the human brain. For example, when seeing someone experience disgust, your neurons fire in the same pattern as when you experience disgust. Given that our neurological system is the underlying infrastructure for thought, this suggests mirroring enables us to empathically reconstruct other peoples' state of mind. We are wired for empathy. Mirror neurons provide scientific evidence for the importance of empathy in our teamwork and leadership behavior.

EMPATHY IN LEADERSHIP

Author of the seminal book, *Emotional Intelligence*, Daniel Goleman has done pioneering work in the role of empathy in leadership. His definition of emotional intelligence (EI) as the essential condition of leadership has become widespread. Based on his research, he claims that IE has "proved to be twice as important as [technical skills or IQ] *for jobs at all levels*" (italics added).

He describes EI as comprising five main elements:

1. **Self-awareness.** Knowing one's strengths, weaknesses, drives, values, and impact on others
2. **Self-regulation.** Controlling or redirecting disruptive impulses and moods
3. **Motivation.** Relishing achievement for its own sake
4. **Empathy.** Understanding other peoples' emotional makeup and state of mind
5. **Social skill.** Building rapport with others to move as a team in desired directions.

Goleman was one of the first to open up the domain of the *emotional life* of the team for conscious practice.

In using these elements across a range of businesses and circumstances, we've come to see a deeper relationship among these five components of EI. While each component involves relatedness, and some operate in parallel, they all depend upon the presence of empathy. The core skill needed for competent leadership, the skill that is the overall integrating factor of the other four elements of EI, is empathy.

Also, as Goleman elaborates in a blog post on www.danielgole man.info, how a leader demonstrates empathy in delivering information is critical. He describes a meeting in which the leader said:

> I've got bad news. Upper management told me this team's performance is unacceptable. We have to pull up our numbers by the end of this quarter, or heads will roll. I've decided to make major changes. First, all vacations for the rest of the quarter are canceled. I expect each of you to be here focused on work. Second, you will meet your weekly goals, no matter how many hours it takes.

Missing from the leader's delivery were the very elements of EI—and any semblance of empathy for team members. You can imagine the distress they felt and how their motivation might have pitched downward as a result. Given how important empathy is within the context of collaboration practice, how can we develop an empathic mindset?

EVOLVING AN EMPATHIC MINDSET

While the idea of empathy in leadership, or the role of myth in teamwork, seem exotic initially, we are not the first to perceive the benefits of an empathic, collaborative mindset. Over 200 years ago, Benjamin Franklin identified aspects of his behavior in need of improvement and wrote in his *Autobiography*:

> I made it a Rule to forbear all direct Contradiction to the Sentiments of others, and all positive Assertion of my own. I even forbid myself ... the Use of every Word or Expression in

the Language that imported a fix'd Opinion; such as *certainly*, *undoubtedly*, &c. and I adopted instead of them, *I conceive, I apprehend,* or *I imagine* a thing to be so or so it appears to me at present.

When another asserted something that I thought an Error, I deny'd my self the Pleasure of contradicting him abruptly, and of showing immediately some Absurdity in his Proposition; and in answering I began by observing that in certain Cases or Circumstances his Opinion would be right, but that in the present case there *appear'd* or *seem'd* to me some Difference, &c.

And this Mode, which I at first put on, with some violence to natural Inclination, became at length so easy & so habitual to me, that perhaps for these Fifty Years past no one has ever heard a dogmatical Expression escape me.

For I was a bad Speaker, ... and yet I carried my Points.

In this short extract, Franklin captures much of the essence of this approach to empathic, creative collaboration.

- He advocates exercising self-control in avoiding either/or thinking and dogmatic expression ("I even forbid myself..." and "...there appear'd or seem'd to me some Difference...").
- He resists the emotional temptation to judge and dominate ("I deny'd my self the Pleasure of contradicting him abruptly...").
- He makes it a point to first acknowledge something about the other person's point of view. Make that acknowledgment *out loud*. Saying this out loud commits you to a more conciliatory position, and is *experienced by the ego as a defeat*, which may be why it's so difficult for some people. But the acknowledgment is experienced by most listeners as a bid for collaboration and establishes a less defensive tone to the conversation moving forward.
- Franklin recognizes that this "Mode" requires a bit of getting used to. Although it does take time and practice, over time it

does become "so habitual" that you will likely notice using it in all forms of communication, not just in business.

- He realizes the benefit from the method that enabled him to carry his points. Franklin may have understated his abilities as a speaker, but his lessons remain useful today. The principle of empathy, practiced authentically, can help improve leadership and team effectiveness.

While what Franklin wrote may seem stilted today, perhaps in our current "evolved" state we have lost something important. Franklin consciously undertook the task of self-improvement and enlisted his well-known discipline and attention to detail to help him achieve his goal. If those traits are not your strong suit, how can you improve your capacity and practice of empathy over time?

Another closely related skill is the ability to freely admit when you are wrong. Michel Eyquem de Montaigne, a 16th-century French philosopher, said it well in "On the Education of Children":

> Make him understand, that to acknowledge the error he shall discover in his own argument, though only found out by himself, is an effect of the judgment and sincerity, which are the principal things he should seek after; that obstinance and contention are common qualities, most appearing in mean souls; that to revise and correct himself, to forsake an unjust argument in the height and heat of dispute, are rare, great, and philosophical qualities.

GAUGING AND IMPROVING YOUR EMPATHY

To be truly empathic, you must be present and reliably so. It requires practice and awareness. There are certain signs, which you can easily monitor, that indicate you are not being empathic:

- **Feeling competitive.** Even if you begin by being open to hearing another person, you may start to feel that the other person is refusing to hear your point of view, prompting you to reassert yours more forcefully.

- **Feeling distracted.** You notice your mind is wandering and you are losing track of what the other person is saying.
- **The other person gets frustrated.** An empathic connection usually leads to a sense of relaxation and ease on the other person's part. Sensing increasing frustration probably means you got off track along the way.
- **Interrupting the other person.** You may find it difficult to stifle the impulse to re-enter the discussion even when the other person is talking.
- **Facial expression/body language.** It has been claimed that in face-to-face conversations more than 90% of the communication consists of non-verbal or paralinguistic cues. In this world of digital communication—email, text, and instant messaging—we dramatically reduce our ability to communicate, particularly if we have never had a face-to-face interaction with the other person. It takes much more effort to avoid miscommunication in cyberspace.
- **Tone.** This clue is even present in telephone conversations. "Tone" here could also mean punctuation in texts, word choices in email, and similar.
- **Resistance felt in body.** This is probably the best measure of attunement or connection. Checking in on physical sensation can provide an early clue to non-connection. Videoconferencing presents special challenges. For example, a delayed response due to video transmission may cause the person to be viewed as slow. Lip movements not synchronized with speech due to video compression may cause the person to be viewed as less credible. And difficulties with eye contact due to camera placement may cause the person to be viewed as unfriendly. Also, some people display "video anxiety" when seeing themselves in a video conference (or FaceTime) session.

What do you do to correct a communication mishap? First, to make sure you aren't jumping to conclusions, ask yourself, "What did I not hear?" Then ask it of others, with a request for a clarification or for a repeat of the statement. If you were distracted, admit it. People appreciate an admission of distraction and are willing to forgive and move on: "I'm sorry. My mind wandered there a bit. Can you please repeat what you were saying?"

We can now see how empathy is the "master emotion" and the main driver behind Emotional Intelligence. Let's relate empathy to the other four dimensions of EI listed earlier.

1. **Self-awareness.** An empathic connection with others supplements self-appraisal with real-world input about how others see you.
2. **Self-regulation.** Empathy enables openness, and openness to change is critical to effective self-regulation.
3. **Motivation.** Empathy is a cornerstone in building and leading teams.
4. **Empathy.**
5. **Social skill.** Empathy is also key to building rapport with others to move them in desired directions.

Empathy draws people together. Think of it as the organizational analogy of a gravitational attractor.

CHAPTER 16

BEYOND EMOTIONAL INTELLIGENCE

Emotional Integrity

E motional intelligence is important. But is it enough? Emotional *integrity* goes beyond emotional intelligence.

Much of business literature on integrity strictly views it from an ethical standpoint. These accounts often seem dry and boring. In contrast John Beebe, a Jungian analyst and former president of the C. G. Jung Institute of San Francisco, views integrity from a psychological perspective. He points out that the result of living "in" integrity is experienced as joy—and the warning signal that we've slipped "out of" integrity is anxiety. Beebe states that "… integrity cannot survive without an attitude of vigilance, and we are always, in effect, restoring our integrity from some attempt at compromise." This, he explains, is the reason that both Confucius and Socrates "urged that we continually question ourselves." Beebe elaborates, saying that we should "consider that the part of ourselves that worries may be the healthy part, the strength of our moral fiber. When this part suffers anxiety, the signal is not wrong, it is telling us that our integrity is somehow at risk."

Integrity is at risk in organizations. Frequently, there is a huge disparity between what is asserted by the team as their values—perhaps as a Code of Ethics plastered on the conference room wall—and the actual behavior in the room. Reducing that disparity occurs when *leadership makes an unconditional commitment to a rigorous and consistent application of these principles and practices.* Unfortunately, such commitments are rare. Leaders often prefer to retain the prerogative to keep their options open, or don't fully grasp how their inconsistencies degrade team performance.

The founder of Bridgewater Associates, one of the world's largest hedge funds, maintains that one of the firm's core operating principles is "radical transparency" with respect to employee grievances and concerns. If, in theory, transparency sounds good, then should radical transparency be potentially even better? Apparently not, for what it meant in practice was a culture of videotaping confrontations between employees—and sharing them with managers, thus creating an oppositional and toxic atmosphere.

In a 2016 complaint, one employee described the firm as a "cauldron of fear and intimidation." (The complainant was not alone in these concerns: Numerous other employees independently reiterated the assertions about the culture of surveillance and intimidation.) According to a *New York Times* article in July of 2016, "an atmosphere of constant surveillance by video and recordings of all meetings—and the presence of patrolling security guards—silences employees who do not fit the Bridgewater mold."

How exactly can a principle of "radical transparency" coexist with the long-standing (and assuredly not transparent) policies that Bridgewater employees must sign confidentiality agreements upon being hired and that they must settle disputes through binding arbitration? Just who is being served here? Clearly, the principle and the policies fostered a negative culture. And, given that "radical transparency" was one of more than 200 principles espoused by the founder, we can imagine that not enough attention was paid to any one principle.

One would like to think that the troubles at Bridgewater were an exception. But change comes slowly. And, for all its faults, there is much to be learned from the Bridgewater example. After all, how can people operate within a culture that does not feel safe? The short answer: not well. The rising generation, having been reared amid the Internet storm and the onslaught of anonymous bullying online, is particularly attuned to the problem of hostile environments. As open and safe cultural alternatives become more widespread and available, it will be increasingly difficult to compete for skilled talent.

CHAPTER 17

COLLABORATION: HOW TO DO EMPATHY

Empathy/Challenge

The process of Empathy/Challenge requires practice to mold it into engrained habit. The effort is worth it, for the process is highly effective.

- **Establish Willingness for Dialogue.** Avoid declarations such as, "We have to talk," which tend to generate resistance. If the listener interprets that request as discussing an unwanted topic, his preferred response might be "No, we don't." Better to initiate the conversation with, "Can we take a moment to discuss your forecast?" It's much harder psychologically to reject that request.

- **Listen with Empathy.** One party listens to the other's explanation without interrupting, attempting during this process to understand rather than to refute the other's point of view. Empathy enters the conversation here.

- **Acknowledge Understanding.** The listener acknowledges *out loud* his or her understanding of at least some part of the other person's position. This acknowledgment can take any of multiple forms. A few examples:
  - "That's a good idea. I hadn't thought of that before."
  - "That's an interesting point of view."
  - "I hear what you say."
  - "I can see why you feel that way."
  - "I can see how that would affect you."
- **Complementarity in Dialogue.** The listener then presents his or her position from a *both/and* instead of an *either/or* perspective. Avoiding either/or thinking and the words that reflect it—*"but"* or *"you're wrong"* or *"agree to disagree"*—may initially require some effort and practice. The objective at this point is to avoid dialogue-ending, ego-based oppositional dialogue. As one colleague mentioned, "When the undiscussable becomes undiscussable, the dialogue must revert to win-lose." What we seek, and what with effort is possible in most cases, is win-win.
- **Extend the Dialogue.** A dialogue ensues, with a back-and-forth exchange. If one party regresses to dogmatically defending their *a priori* position, the other party should encourage a return to empathic dialogue. With its insistence on authentic listening, this process can be quite powerful and constructive.

The first part, Empathy, involves establishing a two-way empathic connection that avoids ego-based oppositional dialogue in favor of two minds open to dialogue, undistracted by *a priori* positions. The goal is to have both points of view held simultaneously by both persons. Participants may need to encourage each other to avoid slipping back into a defensive posture. The focus moves from striving to "win" an argument to agreeing to collaboratively examine a common problem and explore potential solutions acceptable to both parties. It requires *actually listening to and understanding each other.* This process is situated between the methods of Active Listening, where one party simply repeats what the other said, and Constructive Confrontation, where both parties strongly advocate their individual viewpoint.

How does this play out in the real world? About a decade ago, early in our partnership, Howard Teich and I were working with a CEO who was having problems with the vice president of business development, a high-powered executive with business training at Harvard. Though she had previously been enormously effective, she was now going through a divorce, losing focus on her work, and spending a significant portion of her time speaking with her attorney with her office door left open. Her side of those conversations was loud enough to be heard throughout much of the office.

The CEO was clearly apprehensive about the prospect of a confrontation with her and asked for help in planning how to address the matter. We used role playing (a very effective training method), asking the CEO to adopt the role of the VP while we played his role:

TEICH IN THE ROLE OF CEO: I've noticed you've been a bit distracted recently. Would you be willing to talk about how this is playing out in the company? (Eliciting willingness)

CEO IN THE ROLE OF VP: Sure. (Hard to say "No" to)

TEICH IN THE ROLE OF CEO: It seems that personal issues have leaked into your job performance and the staff is a bit frustrated with the distraction. (Expressed as a concern instead of as an accusation)

CEO IN THE ROLE OF VP: Well, you know I have made great contributions to the company, and you even gave me that award last year for bringing in a critical partner. (First line of defense)

TEICH IN THE ROLE OF CEO: You are absolutely right. You did make an important contribution back then and were recognized for it. (Empathy and agreement with something about her position) Now (not "But"), I believe the current issues need resolution for the benefit of the company, and I really want you

to show up in this conversation and work with me on this matter.
(Challenge)

This example illustrates the Empathy/Challenge cycle, which (contrary to some people's initial impression) does not tiptoe around the problem. It can be direct, persistent, and effective—even as it addresses awkward issues with sensitivity.

Notice the power of role-playing. The CEO had no idea how to deal effectively with this problem, yet was obsessing over it. Role-playing was like turning on the lights and walking him through the process; the role-play demonstrated the general concept while providing a script.

The VP agreed to the CEO's request for a conversation, passed through moments of defensiveness, and then conceded her contribution to the problem.

Not all matters will be resolved in a single conversation. If necessary, it might be productive to take a break and let concerns stew without "agreeing to disagree." Sometimes it takes time for the heat of conflict to cook a new solution.

Dr. Peter M. Rojcewicz, Provost at the Pacifica Graduate Institute, provides an apt metaphor for collaboration. He likens the practice to improvisation. Here, one participant offers a riff and the other builds on it. This continues back and forth until something new emerges: a new creation.

Four rules for improvisation have been provided on zapier.com:

Rule 1. Say Yes.
Rule 2. Say Yes AND.
Rule 3. Make Statements.
Rule 4. There Are No Mistakes.

COLLABORATION AND CONSENSUS

We often run across confusion regarding the practice of consensus. It is frequently mistaken for majority rule, which it is not. The classic definition of consensus is that 1) everyone gets to offer his or her perspective, and 2) the decision is explained. This marries collaboration dialogue with top-down leadership in an effective manner and sets up clear expectations for the team regarding decision-making.

CHAPTER 18

MARKETING AND EMPATHY

Real Marketing

I f the very idea of putting the words marketing and empathy together in one sentence, much less making it the focus of an entire chapter, triggers some dissonance in your mind, you're not alone.

Dinesh D'Souza makes an interesting case for capitalism in his book *America: Imagine a World Without Her*. He points out that "success under capitalism comes not through self-absorption but by attending to the wants and needs of others." That is, understanding how to please the consumer. This entails empathy and is an important skill (or virtue) for us to encourage and support. Again.

D'Souza takes us back over 250 years to Adam Smith, considered to be the founder of classical free market economic theory. Smith is most famous for his seminal work *An Inquiry into the Nature and Causes of the Wealth of Nations* (1776). Less well-known is the fact that he made empathy the central theme of his earlier book, *A Theory of Moral Sentiments* (1759). As D'Souza explains, "Smith made a surprising observation 'To feel much for others, and little for yourselves, to restrain our selfish, and indulge our benevolent, affections constitutes the perfection of human nature.'" D'Souza then points out that "This is precisely what successful workers and entrepreneurs do. They put themselves in the place of others. They ask: how can I provide a service that is really helpful to other people? How can I develop and provide my products so they better meet with the consumers' want?"

As an indicator of the significance of this discussion, notice its persistence across four centuries, from Smith in the 18th to D'Souza in the 21st!

Some readers may feel incredulous at the idea of capitalism being driven by empathy. Isn't capitalism really about greed? But if empathy is "the ability to identify with or understand another's situation or feelings," then isn't that what effective marketing is all about? Haven't the most successful entrepreneurs delivered products that anticipated customer interests and feelings? How did they succeed if not by first imagining themselves to be in the customers' shoes? Also, in what might be called *anticipated empathy*, entrepreneurs often create products before users even conceive of their possibility. Here, we have another case of complementarity: Profit motive often drives entrepreneurial action, while empathy provides an important connection to the customer. D'Souza argues that "capitalism civilizes greed," with empathy as its virtuous companion.

CAPITAL M MARKETING

Especially in the high-tech industry, marketing often seems like the lesser function, the sideshow to product design. We have always promoted "Capital M marketing," marketing taken seriously. Capital M marketing requires ingenuity and sustained effort to pull off.

Just as there is a mandate for a new type of leadership, we foresee a parallel mandate for this stronger form of marketing. Marketing, like effective team leadership, becomes an important competitive advantage. Just as collaborative leadership requires new principles and practices (as described in this book), similar factors enable a shift toward Capital M marketing as the leading edge in future organizations. That shift in perspective demands work—and time.

Typically, one needs several months after coming into a company to achieve a cultural breakthrough. Implementing a Capital M marketing program requires tapping into the deep creative consciousness of a connected team. The team needs dialogue to achieve creative outcomes. Too often, startups, deeply enamored with their technology, underestimate the effort needed to define the marketing function in the company.

I recently saw this yet again with a startup that spent years developing a full spectrum of intellectual property (IP). The founder assumed he could figure out the marketing strategy and positioning in one month. Marketing had only minor input into product development, yet marketing was necessary to create the crucial link to future customers. The technologists' view of this just being a simple process respects neither the difficulty nor the value of doing it right. Why? Perhaps because marketing has an ineffable quality to it and is therefore suspect.

CREATIVE CONSCIOUSNESS IN THE TEAM

What does the process for tapping into the deep creative consciousness of an effective marketing team look like? The following is a suggested approach.

Train the Team on the Principles and Practices

Set up the underlying ground rules for dialogue before embarking on a marketing and positioning process. These rules will enable the team members to confront and defuse resistance that may arise along the way.

For example, in one company, the lead marketing executive persisted in putting up roadblocks every step of the way. He would allow the creative process involving executives and key influencers to reach a tentative outcome, and then declare the result impossible to implement. Somehow, it was always too controversial, not sufficiently defensible, or simply not to his liking. In fact, his thinly disguised opposition to effectively positioning the company and its products stemmed from the unwelcome light this initiative placed on the executive's prior failure to execute a key marketing task.

We got past his resistance by using the collaborative dialogue approach and reaffirmed the team consensus. As a result, for the first time in its history, the company had a website that explained clearly what the company was doing. Shortly thereafter, the executive left the company on his own initiative.

Explain Positioning and Motivate the Process

Some teams have little or no experience with marketing, and most teams have unequal expertise in the practice. Carl Jung said one of the central problems in marriage is that each party believes the other party has the same psychology as their own. So it goes with teams, especially in technology. If we think our technology is cool, so must everybody else. Rarely is there acknowledgment that, to succeed in the marketplace, the company must speak in the frame of reference of the *customer* (rather than of the *company* in its self-infatuation).

In a recent a conversation, the suggestion was made to "feature our location." I replied, "That's about us. What about them?" In other words, "So what? What's the benefit to the customer of our location?" In this case, they *did* have a great location for delivering their services, but nobody would come there unless convinced that deeper, and more relevant, benefits were made clear. If the location is wildly convenient to the main consumers, it might be relevant—if so stated. But, given the Internet's reach, physical location is often irrelevant. So you might consider this step as a move in the direction of corporate empathy and away from corporate narcissism.

To reinforce the point, consider the following:

According to a June 21, 2016, *Wall Street Journal* article by Joann S. Lublin entitled "Companies Try a New Strategy: Empathy

Training," an increasing number of businesses are focusing on empathy in developing managers and products.

In a study assessing more than 15,000 leaders in 18 countries, the human-resources consultancy Development Dimensions International found that those "who master listening and responding to others are the most successful leaders." Simply put, empathy training improves the bottom line. How? Contemporary workers want to feel connected and work with others, including bosses, who are "attuned to their feelings." According to the study, "The top 10 businesses among 160 in a 2015 Global Empathy Index generated 50% more net income per employee than the bottom 10." How companies treat workers and communicate with customers clearly makes a difference.

At least two automobile companies—Aston Martin Lagonda Ltd., a British sports car maker, and Ford—have taken empathy to heart in an effort to attract more female buyers. Soon after joining design teams at Ford, new (never pregnant) engineers must simulate pregnancy. By strapping on a weighted "empathy belly" they experience the extra pounds, back pain, and bladder pressure familiar to pregnant women everywhere. This enables engineers to better appreciate some of the challenges of pregnancy. Even their brief experience has influenced ergonomic features in certain models, such as easier automatic adjustments of the driver's seat.

Some employers require supervisors to update their empathy skills regularly. As Dennis DiMaggio, chief learning officer at Breakthru Beverage explains, "Empathy is chess, not checkers. It takes a while to develop that skill." And it takes practice, in all venues.

Work Through the Message Architecture Process
(see the next section)
This process can be difficult and require multiple iterations. Accept the creative tension and don't let anyone shut down the process prematurely, which they might attempt in order to avoid effort or

discomfort. Keep the focus on the view from the outside in. The need for an outside-in focus was illustrated in a company that had recently been formed through four acquisitions. For quite a while, their positioning was "We do A, B, C, and D. Really well." The (apparently unexplored and) unanswered question was "What does this add up to?" another variation on "So what?" The company's statement was rather like saying "We sell pansies, roses, daisies, and violets" rather than "We are a specialty florist." The message architecture process can help.

Field Test the Results

This is where detachment helps. Be prepared to toss out the current version and seek a better approach. In one case, we were positioning an advanced networking product as "scalable bandwidth to the desktop" (never mind what that means, it was an accurate description of what the product did—and one that would be familiar to the intended purchasers). Once launched, sales increased at a modest rate. Based on customer feedback, we then changed our description to "collapsed backbone." (This actually meant something in network terms, although it sounds to an outsider like an orthopedic catastrophe.) Sales accelerated dramatically. Same product, same technology, different description.

Our collaborative leadership method is ideal for creating a strong marketing presence. An exceptional promise can radiate through all levels of the organization to the customer, the appropriate ultimate beneficiary of the promise. Focusing on truth, reliability, and value provides a strong basis for creating a Capital M marketing company. Now, how do we get there?

EMPATHY IN MARKETING—AND IN THE MESSAGE ARCHITECTURE

To further examine the role of empathy in marketing, let's examine the concept of message architecture, an important discipline for developing marketing messages for products, services—and even companies at large. The basic approach is illustrated in Figure 18-1.

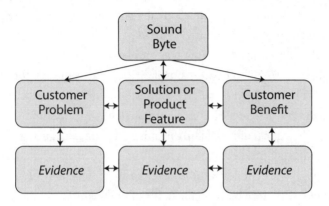

FIGURE 18-1 Message Architecture

The top-level message, or sound byte ("byte" being a nod to its frequent tech-company usage) summarizes the message in a short descriptive phrase. For American Express it's "Don't Leave Home Without It."

The process begins with defining the customer problem, proceeds to identifying the solution or feature being offered that can solve the problem, and concludes by articulating the customer benefit. So far, so good. The real work comes in supporting each set of claims with evidence. Evidence can be in the form of facts, examples, benchmarks, logical arguments, quotes, and more. The requirement for evidence imposes rigor on the marketing process, because claims made without evidence might simply be untrue and, even if true, lack credibility. Aside from the ethical problem, false claims don't work very well or for very long.

When implemented successfully, the messaging architecture process provides a core set of messages that can be used in all marketing material. The message architecture itself is rarely presented to external audiences. Instead, it remains behind the scenes as a foundation to ensure message relevance, coherence, and consistency.

What does empathy have to do with all this? Empathy exerts its influence in two ways. Most importantly, it insists on a thorough understanding of the customer problem, itself a direct act of empathy. Then, it insists on an explanation of customer benefit, grounded in solid evidence to avoid inflated claims.

Sounds great, right? Now the problem. Message architecture is very hard to implement in a normal team environment for several reasons. First, it is hard work. A team might well spend an entire day just to draft a first version for one product. Second, and more importantly, this work requires a shift in mindset, from imagining marketing as a purely intellectual activity to one involving relatedness and empathy. It means taking the trouble to form deep and illuminating dialogues with real customers. It means not simply tossing off the messaging task as an intellectual simulation of customer interest but taking the time and making the effort to establish a deep connection with the customer.

LEAN STARTUP AND DESIGN THINKING

As founders seek faster and more efficient ways to launch businesses, several new movements have arisen. One is the Lean Startup (see theleanstartup.com), viewing a business plan as a set of *hypotheses* versus a plan to be executed. The focus of a Lean Startup is on developing a Minimum Viable Product (MVP) tested with early customers for feedback. If tests indicate that the product design is off target, the company then "pivots" to the next iteration, until an acceptable product design is reached. Then, and only then, does the company scale to operation.

Another is Design Thinking, a concept pursued in the Stanford Graduate School of Business. Design Thinking features a user-centered approach to product conception and design. It begins with deep immersion in the customer's world. Design Thinking is sometimes considered as oppositional to the engineering emphasis of Lean Startups. They are in fact fundamentally similar approaches, both seeking a lower risk path to meeting customer needs through innovation.

For our purposes, what is interesting about these two approaches is that they are both firmly anchored in the principles and practices in this book. That is, these are examples of how our approach is not just a new method, but a *generator* of methods, across all types of businesses, not just startups. Consider: Both Lean Startup and Design Thinking involve a kind of forced march to *empathy*. The Lean Startup relies heavily on the mindset dimensions of *agility* and *relatedness* (with some *courage* and *awareness* mixed in). Both rely on *nonattachment* to set aside initial expectations and entertain the possibility of a better idea, and they share a fundamental respect for complementarity by explicitly integrating external customer needs with internal business goals. At the heart of both is *collaboration* with prospective customers, and presumably among team members.

Since its inception around 2008, the Lean Startup has generated a huge amount of interest, with thousands of seminars, articles, case studies, and even academic appointments. Yet there seems to be a tad bit of inflation as well, a sense that this breakthrough revolutionizes startup methodologies permanently. One senses an emerging counterargument, that customers really don't want to waste their time talking with a bunch of wild-eyed entrepreneurs, that sometimes lean isn't enough and full product functionality is necessary to gain customer interest. The Fat Startup may be waiting offstage for its proper reintroduction. The pendulum swings, and in the unrelenting pursuit of competitive advantage, the beat goes on.

CHAPTER 19

NONATTACHMENT

Enabling Creative Dialogue

Nonattachment—"lack of emotion or of personal interest"—is one of three foundational principles in our method, alongside empathy and complementarity. Being nonattached is different from being detached: "separated or disconnected." Being nonattached means being observant, attentive, and concerned with the matter at hand, whereas being detached means not being connected to it at all.

Why would nonattachment be an important principle? Isn't passion a treasured quality in a team, the common determination to "change the world"? Certainly, but that's different. You can be passionate about something without being possessed by it. That's inflation, which we will revisit shortly. You can passionately aspire to climb a mountain, but also be clear-eyed about the challenges and dangers along the way, rather than acting precipitously.

We employ nonattachment to provide a clear perception of reality, to maintain creative flow, avoiding rigid dogmatic thinking. Nonattachment in many ways resembles what the poet John Keats describes as "negative capability" … "that is when man is capable of being in uncertainties. Mysteries, doubts, without any irritable reaching after fact and reason." Keats' point of view refutes attempts to categorize all experience into an official epistemology (theory of knowledge). Instead, Keats advocates tolerating uncertainty and deferring premature conclusions as prerequisites of the mindset conducive to creative collaboration.

An analogy from quantum theory is the phenomenon of the quantum vacuum state that declares the impossibility of a perfect vacuum—rather, it is one where energy and particles spontaneously appear and disappear. Holding the creative void in dialogue without attachments likewise yields spontaneous ideas and concepts.

In particular, we deploy nonattachment as a defense against idealized expectations, inflation, hubris, and illusion, what we might call the Four Horsemen of the Apocalypse when it comes to mindset. These four are closely associated, but often distinct in their manifestation. We will start our analysis at the source of these counterproductive mental states—narcissism.

In any team or group situation, we need to get our egos and our idealized expectations out of the way to really understand others (and accurately sense how others understand us). Examining the myth of Narcissus can lead us to a better understanding of the need for, and the advantages of, nonattachment.

To promote nonattachment, it is helpful to understand the concept of psychological projection. Formally, projection is defined as "the attribution of one's own attitudes, feelings, or desires to someone or something." We project our unacknowledged thoughts or feelings onto others. Projection is an automatic, unconscious process. It is not something we intend; it is something that just happens. And, as Jung explains, being projected on by another leaves you with a heavy feeling. In organizations, projection keeps us from understanding each other, instead (unconsciously) preferring to believe we know the other person's mindset. Meanwhile, the recipient (the projectee, if you will) experiences projection as frustration. It is exasperating to be in a dialogue where you don't seem to be seen or heard and are misrepresented.

To recognize these feelings, imagine yourself calling a business or a computer support line. In a *New York Times* article on "Why Tech Support Is (Purposely) Unbearable," Kate Murphy wrote of the frustration we've all experienced, which she refers to as "tech support rage." Whether we're talking to a computer or a person who is confined to a script, we feel as though we have no influence on the conversation. As Art Markman, professor of psychology at the University of Texas at Austin, explained to the *New York Times* in 2016, if the computer or the person replies in a way that is non-responsive or that

> "makes no sense, now I see that all these words I spoke have had no effect whatsoever on what's happening here." When things don't make sense and feel out of control, mental health experts say, humans instinctively feel threatened. Though you would like to think you can employ reason in this situation, you're really just a mass of neural impulses and primal reactions. Think fight or flight, but you can't do either because you are stuck on the phone, which provokes rage.

Despite past experience, some part of you may hold the idealized expectation that the process will improve, and that next time you call you'll be directed to an actual person who is helpful and knowledgeable. Someone who can help solve the problem. Perhaps in your less optimistic (or more realistic) moments, you'd recognize this as an idealized fantasy. That's a step, and an important one.

Granted, tech support rage is its own special hell. But ratchet that down a few notches and you have a sense of what recipients of projection feel. Imagine attempting to collaborate with someone who stays on script and ignores new ideas. If your teammate isn't responsive, not being heard can feel like an insult and result in discomfort, anger, and resentment.

To understand the phenomenon of projection, let's again dip momentarily into the mythic layer and examine the story of Narcissus.

THE MYTH OF NARCISSUS

The origin of the myth of Narcissus goes back over two thousand years, with the classic version from Book III of *Metamorphoses* by Ovid (43 BC to 17/18 AD). You may be familiar with the portion of the myth that tells of Narcissus gazing at his own reflection. This myth will warn us that narcissism is a commonplace and continuing feature of humanity. We should be prepared for it to influence teamwork and leadership.

. . .

According to the myth, Narcissus was an exceptionally proud youth renowned for his beauty. At the young age of 16, many "youths and young girls" fell in love with him, but because of his intense pride, none affected him and he rejected all who approached. One was Echo, an attractive mountain nymph who had been quite a chatterbox. She got into trouble with Hera, Zeus's wife, when she was found out to have been distracting Hera with mindless conversation to keep Hera from investigating one of Zeus's recent escapades. As punishment, Hera took away Echo's voice so that she could only repeat what others said aloud. As Ovid put it, Echo "cannot be silent when others have spoken, nor learn how to speak first herself." This doesn't make for a great conversationalist, but you might imagine how it would appeal to Narcissus.

And so it went. One day, Echo sees Narcissus and falls immediately in love. Thanks to the punishment, she cannot call out to him, but can only utter the last words she hears another speak. Thinking the footfalls he hears are his lost hunting companions, Narcissus calls out, "Is anyone here?" and hears Echo's reply of "Here." Eventually he calls, "Here, let us meet together."

Echo, deliriously happy, replies "Together" and throws herself on him. This angers Narcissus. As has been his pattern with suitors, he rejects Echo, saying, "Hands off! I would rather die than you should have me!" In the process, he throws her to the ground. Brokenhearted, Echo runs off to the mountains and eventually wastes away, leaving behind only her voice that repeats what others say.

The gods, including Nemesis, the goddess of divine vengeance, were displeased by Narcissus's behavior. They arranged that the only one he would love could never love him back. One day, a tired and thirsty Narcissus came upon a bright pool of water. In drinking from it, he caught a reflection in the still water and was instantly smitten. In a section of Ovid's *Metamorphosis* called Narcissus's Lament (as translated by Addison), we see Narcissus's confusion and distress as he confronts someone who for the first time doesn't pursue him (as noted in italics in the following excerpt, which are added).

> And yet the lovely mimick wears a face
> That kindly smiles, and when I bend to join
> My lips to his, he fondly bends to mine.
> Hear, gentle youth, and pity my complaint,
> Come from thy well, thou fair inhabitant.
> My charms an easy conquest have obtain'd
> O'er other hearts, *by thee alone disdain'd*.
> But why should I despair? I'm sure he burns
> With equal flames, and languishes by turns.
> When-e'er I stoop, he offers at a kiss,
> And when my arms I stretch, he stretches his.
> His eye with pleasure on my face he keeps,
> He smiles my smiles, and when I weep he weeps.
> When e'er I speak, his moving lips appear
> To utter something, which I cannot hear.

In this passage, the poet has created a stunning example of distortion and self-centeredness. Narcissus is confident that the other is burning "with equal flames" and therefore that he himself need not "despair." And yet he is simply projecting his own state of mind on another person—who is (as we know) not another person but simply his reflection. This is a case of projection, where an observer believes something about someone else that is actually in the observer's mind. Ovid here is supremely ironic: This is perhaps a singular example of a projection being accurate in that what Narcissus actually sees is himself, and yet still remains hopelessly wrong about what constitutes reality.

In time, Narcissus realizes

It is myself I love, myself I see;
The gay delusion is a part of me.

At the end of the myth, Narcissus either dies or withers away (depending on the version you read) much as Echo did. But instead of a voice remaining, Narcissus is replaced by the narcissus flower, or daffodil, with white petals surrounding a yellow heart.

CHAPTER 20

LESSONS FROM NARCISSUS

Dangers of Self-Centeredness in the Team

N arcissus taught us to be less charmed by beauty and outward appearance, and be more attentive to events outside our ego-limited realm of consciousness. For leadership, the myth of Narcissus seems more a warning than a model. We can infer from the myth how narcissism bogs things down. It degrades communication because so often the communication is about the person, not the current team reality. It injects skepticism into commitment when we know what the other person's priority really is: himself or herself. Collaboration is encumbered by the additional step of getting the other side off their self-centeredness and onto the matter at hand. And it becomes the inferior dimension—Relatedness—at the Mindset layer, the gateway through which inflation, hubris, idealized fantasies, and illusion enter the system. Narcissism is the enemy of urgency. It is the sand in the gears for creating the deeply connected team.

The story of Narcissus sharpens our lens. Once we accept the myth's lesson that narcissism is a universal part of our humanity, we can detect it early … and often. It is a red flag for team evolution, and a useful factor in interviewing candidates. Self-centeredness can be a sign of someone trying to make up an alternative persona, the opposite of the general idea of hiring people who are "comfortable in their own skin."

The myth warns about the grip of narcissism. Narcissus could not change: a warning to what may happen on the team.

The story of Narcissus also warns us that the self-centered leader will not receive input, preferring to continue operating on his or her superior perception of reality. Narcissus could neither change nor evolve. He didn't ignore the call to evolution, because he never heard it. In this sense, narcissism also diminishes Awareness, cutting off the critical flow of vital external and internal information. Perhaps that is the biggest lesson from the myth, and the warning that keeps us from turning into a planted flower.

Narcissism is thus not just annoying, but dangerous. Self-centeredness also seems to be widespread, nearly an epidemic. David McCullough, Pulitzer Prize–winner and famous national historian, makes a plea for a different attitude in *The American Spirit*. "John Adams, a Founding Father of America and its 2nd President, wrote to his wife Abigail at home, 'We can't guarantee success [in the war] but we can do something better. We can deserve it.' Think how different that is from the attitude today when all that matters for far too many is success, being number one, getting ahead, getting to the top. However you betray or claw or cheat is immaterial if you get to the top." Perhaps that is the call of our leadership method: not to guarantee success, which we have explained depends on many factors outside our control, but to deserve it.

The Narcissus myth dwells on excessive concern with oneself. Narcissus represents an inherent component of the human psyche, which in modest form represents a natural self-interest, but in exaggerated form can lead to psychological isolation or even madness.

In politics, business, and in life, myths help us remember basic truths about human experience and behavior. There is no denying that narcissists and narcissistic attitudes abound in today's world. Depending upon the size of your team, chances are there is at least one narcissist (or someone leaning in that direction). Don't despair; there are solutions.

DETECTING NARCISSISM IN THE TEAM

Many of the myriad forms of mindset dysfunctionality have narcissism as a root cause or, at the very least, have it in a supporting role. Learning to recognize narcissism in the organization, and deal with it effectively, is an important part of teamwork and leadership. How can you develop that skill? There are warning signs—and you can familiarize yourself with them easily.

Warning signs that become increasingly observable in practice (the following is inspired, in part, by referencing the classic symptoms of a Narcissistic Personality Disorder):

- Opinionated personality with a marked refusal to compromise
- Lack of empathy and the capacity to hear another person's point of view
- Frequently uses dogmatic statements ("We have to…")
- Arrogant, resentful, and envious
- An exaggerated sense of self-importance, as if innate superiority takes precedence over achievements and contributions
- Manipulative and exploitive, such as dumping unpleasant tasks on subordinates that should be handled directly
- Strong sense of entitlement
- Requiring excessive admiration: a "high maintenance case"

Once you detect narcissism, the question becomes how to address it. This brings us back to nonattachment, the focus of this chapter.

ELIMINATING NARCISSISM VIA NONATTACHMENT

Indeed, we are promoting an even broader vision that extends beyond the negative effort to eliminate narcissism. We want to maximize the principle and practice of nonattachment in team members. Remember, this is not detachment—being disengaged or aloof, unable (or unwilling) to join with the team effort to implement a vision. Narcissism and the detachment it engenders are major obstacles to creative collaboration and successful execution. By contrast, nonattachment is a form of joint reflective consciousness that prefers reality to fantasy and relies on careful listening and observation to guide decisions and actions.

Winston Churchill, Prime Minister of the United Kingdom, understood before many the threat of Nazi Germany in the 1930s. In the first volume, *The Gathering Storm*, of his history of WWII, Churchill described his speech to Parliament warning against comforting illusions: "We ought to set the life and endurance of the British Empire and the greatness of the Island very high in our duty, and *not be led astray by illusions about an ideal world*, which only means that other and worse controls will step into our place, and that the future direction will belong to them." (italics added) Here we have an example of idealized expectations gripping an entire populace, leading to a regrettable lack of preparation, and thereafter requiring desperate measures to eventually prevail in the ensuing conflict.

Eliminating narcissism from leadership and teamwork goes a long way to clear the path so as to realize the high-performance creativity of the connected team. The objective is that the team be in a constant state of what Mihaly Csikszentmihalyi refers to as flow (some call it "slipstreaming"), constructively dealing with reality as it unfolds and turning unanticipated events into competitive advantages. Part of this requires training team members to incorporate the principles and practices that maximize the potential of creative teamwork to achieve successful outcomes. Make the commitment to introduce and reinforce collaborative principles and practices, use the concept of diplomatic immunity to encourage open communication, employ the Empathy/Response process to recognize and resolve ide-alized fantasies early, and constantly monitor one's own conduct as a team member and team leader. The following is a critical benefit of *Blueprint*: The collective intelligence of the team, dominated by team members not caught in a narcissistic complex, diminishes the effect of narcissism through enlightened perception and superior collaboration.

CHAPTER 21

THE PARADOX OF SUCCESS AND FAILURE

A Redemptive Narrative

One of the main obstacles to change is fear of failure. Terror, actually. We may prefer to remain in our suboptimal but familiar state rather than risk the unknown to an uncertain future. So, it is worth examining success and failure as complementary states with possibly unexpected dimensions.

Success gets much praise and is widely celebrated; failure is often considered an orphan. Even more, in *Things That Matter*, Charles Krauthammer points out the imbalance between success and failure: "In sports, the joy of winning is dwarfed by the pain of losing. Why even play the game? The joy in losing is this: Where there are no expectations, there is no disappointment."

Yet the two interplay and have a mutual dependence. Let's start with the interesting side: failure. Increasingly, failure is being regarded as an essential factor in business, and especially in entrepreneurial life. "Creative Destruction," a concept in economics articulated by the Austrian American economist Joseph Schumpeter, describes the incessant process of industrial evolution in which the old is destroyed and the new created. Often referred to as "Schumpeter's gale," he considered it to be "the essential fact about capitalism." So failure is apparently recognized as wired into the very fabric of business, not just as an accidental side effect, but as a mainstream recurring reality.

The technology sector celebrates the "fail fast" concept in start-ups. Silicon Valley often proudly considers failure as a badge of honor, almost an essential experience in the team as a condition for providing financial support. Yet throughout all this, there is a sense that failure is an intellectually accepted condition, but emotionally remains a shame-inducing stigma. This split, this lack of balance between the opposing poles of success and failure, does not understand the paradoxical nature of failure sometimes as a gift and success as a burden. Failure can defeat our egocentric illusion of power, shatter our attachment to the fantasy of easy outcome, and ground us in the reality of things as preparation for the next go-around. Failure gives weight and heft to our future attempts and induces the adrenaline rush to sustain the effort. Success without encountering the shadow of failure can mean unmoored inflation, with the ego-based conviction of something approaching omnipotence. How many times have we heard stories of the first-time entrepreneur who by sheer serendipity hit it big on his first venture, and then convinced of his own potency, blows it all on his next catastrophic attempt? Attaining the proper relationship to failure is a central theme of this book.

Again, we can refer to the mythic layer for clarity. There is an old Chinese fable about the farmer's son who lost his favorite horse. Bad. Next day the horse returned followed by 12 wild horses. Good. Later the son broke his leg. Bad. But then a war started, and the son escaped losing his life in a hopeless battle. Good. The lesson is that you never know.

Jeffrey Katzenberg headed Disney's motion picture division for 10 years and then got fired. He then teamed with Hollywood heavy-weights Steven Spielberg and David Geffen to launch DreamWorks, where they turned out hits including *Saving Private Ryan*, *Castaway*,

A Beautiful Mind, and *Shrek*. Commenting on this "failure" and the ups and downs of his career, he said "When you're put in the wrong place at the wrong time, you learn amazing things about life, you experience moments of sacrifice, and learn how to be a leader." He also said that managing a company "is about creating a great environment for people to be able to pursue and realize dreams, even though those dreams, in many cases, are anywhere between improbable and impossible."

This book is about the redemptive narrative of learning how to do things better from seeing how they can go badly. Our lives have up and down moments, and when we are down, learning how to get back up and prevail is part of its art form.

CHAPTER 22

IDEALIZED EXPECTATIONS: CANCER OF THE MIND

Roadblock to a Creative Culture

Idealized expectations show up almost automatically in relationships, among individuals or teams. An idealized expectation happens when one person has an ego-based idea of what the other person should do or think. The presumption is that the holder of the expectation knows better than others.

The prevalence of idealized expectations is one of the biggest roadblocks to establishing a highly collaborative culture. Idealized expectations are a near neighbor to, or (perhaps more appropriately) a root cause of dogmatism and either/or thinking, both major obstacles to team cohesion. More broadly, idealized expectations are also the root cause for multiple forms of mindset dysfunctionality, which is why we think of the condition as "cancer of the mind."

We use the term "idealized fantasies" to convey a more pejorative view of idealized expectations, reflecting our frustration concerning its frequent and apparently automatic appearance among teams. How to counteract idealized fantasies? Look to nonattachment.

The underlying principle of nonattachment and the ability of team members and leaders to adopt it is critical to the quality of team performance.

Nonattachment has a side benefit of making the environment more welcoming for the small voice, encouraging input from all quarters, from all levels, whatever the (potential) risk to ego or plan. We've already seen some of the advantages of seeking out and attending to the small voices. The flip side is that ignoring or squelching those voices can have dire consequences.

Let's look at a case study of idealized expectations and the consequence for value creation.

Returning to SCI, the herd of Ph.D. smartasses described in the Preface, it is clear in retrospect that the lack of clear long-term vision for the company meant that it remained stuck in its original state. Ten years later, when I returned to SCI after a year in the Sloan Program at Stanford's Graduate School of Business, I initiated a "strategic management" process, developed with Dan Thomas, to overhaul the company. We were a contract research firm ("Listed under Smarts in the Yellow Pages") identifying and developing new technologies with scalable potential. For example, we would start with a $50,000 contract to develop an analytic method, in one case optimum power flow algorithms in large-scale electric power grids to reduce fuel costs. We would then secure a $500,000 contract for a prototype demonstration, followed by a $5 million to $20 million full-scale implementation. You might call this the "life cycle process for professional services." Once you have packaged a product, other players cannot compete on price (or availability) because they would have to incur the development costs to catch up. You have already incurred those costs, and now can price below development cost and make a profit through incremental sales. The generalized principle is that you can move through the product life cycle at the speed of the industry, or you can train the competition that jumps on the opportunity and takes it forward.

The problem was lack of vision to exploit the principles behind this life-cycle model, instead remaining attached to the contract research model. When the strategic management process identified the potential to scale existing research contracts into incremental business, the CEO quickly produced a list of ten major market opportunities where the company had failed to take advantage of its initial design project. These neglected opportunities totaled hundreds of millions of dollars. However, the insight came too late. By then, the company had been sold for $15 million, not a bad price at that time for a contract research company, but at least an order of magnitude less than could have been achieved. A similar company, Science Applications International Corporation (SAIC), founded within a year of SCI, reached $4.5 billion dollars in revenue in 2013 with 15,000 employees.

In retrospect, SCI leadership had the same opportunity to transform the company into a much bigger and more valuable entity. There were multiple instances where the potential for incremental revenue leveraging already completed research and proven technology came into sight and were not ignored. In fact, several SCI research teams left the company and started a product company due to the refusal of management to pursue compelling market opportunities. The attachment to a comfortable (and increasingly irrelevant) business model combined with a non-collaborative executive team caused the company to miss the boat, over and over.

The idealized expectation here is that the original business model would persist indefinitely, and that the company could rely on that expectation despite evolving external circumstances. "Where there is no vision, the people perish" (Proverbs 29:18). Or, where the only vision is self-absorption, the narcissistic perish.

Nonattachment provides an opportunity to slip the bonds of idealized expectations. Imbedding nonattachment in the culture allows for corrective action to be taken before it is too late, rather than lament the consequences in retrospect.

WILLING BLINDFULNESS

Let's look at some historical instances of idealized fantasies in their various forms observed in the wild. These stories exceed the statute of limitations, and illustrate that leadership dysfunctionality is pervasive across all times.

Inflation

Inflation ("puffed up, empty pretentiousness") is a pernicious condition affecting individuals, teams, communities, and even religious and political movements, usually with disastrous consequences. It is a form of possession, of rationality subjugated by passion. Inflation prohibits the key question that is vital in startups: What are we not thinking of?

The tech community has had its periodic inflation encounters in its bubbles. And those bubbles have been separated by sufficient time that newer participants have not had the learning experience and older ones have had time to forget. One sure diagnostic for being in a bubble is when everyone denies we are in one.

Identifying when one is in an inflation is difficult. To paraphrase Jung, asking to identify the inflation you are in is like trying to see the lion that just ate you. When you are in an inflation, and can recognize it, it is best to exit before the inevitably unpleasant conclusion. If you have trouble recognizing inflation, ask the people around you to bring it to your attention. They probably know well before you do.

One example of inflation from the near past is the computer network supplier Novell as an example of one kind of inflation—in this case, entitlement—run wild. Entitlement emerges from a pernicious combination of denial and narcissism. It seems to evolve in two steps: gain some claim to superiority and then refuse to give it up when circumstances change. Novell fit that pattern well.

Founded in 1979, Novell had initially failed as a microcomputer company, but thrived through the 1980s with its main product, NetWare, a system for providing basic services (print, file, etc.)

across a computer network. Then they ran into strong headwinds with Microsoft's entry in the market with its integrated desktop applications for word-processing, spreadsheets, and presentations.

During the early 1990s, CEO Noorda counterattacked, paying a then eye-popping 1.4 billion dollars in 1994 for the WordPerfect application and acquiring other assets to combat Microsoft on their own turf. His efforts eventually failed. In 1995, Novell revenues peaked at $2 billion, declining in the next year to $1.3 billion, and then to $1 billion the following year. Novell's stock price plummeted, never to recover.

Despite its deteriorating market position, the company was in the grips of a massive entitlement mentality. It was clear that Microsoft had just polished off the company's lunch and had started in on its dinner. Yet people walked around basking in the now diminishing glow of its prior success. Despite multiple attempts to marshal the creative effort to reinvent the company, business as usual prevailed. Even the new CEO, Bob Frankenberg, a highly regarded Hewlett-Packard veteran, made the mistake of leaving in place senior management from the past, when a major shakeup was called for. Attempts to change the culture, such as encouraging open communication, were greeted by comments such as, "If you speak up around here, you get shot." This cultural style could be attributed to the focus on top-down, command and control, hierarchical leadership.

Using our model, one might argue this was simply an Enterprise Layer matter. One company got outflanked by another and lost, part of the ongoing business saga of creative destruction. But is the explanation really that simple, or did an unsavory menu of hubris, entitlement, and suppressive management contribute to the adverse outcome? Expanding markets provide many opportunities for successful business repositioning. The company could have, for example, shed its attachment to past glory and strategy. It might then have anticipated the emerging power of the Internet and leaped forward, potentially outflanking Microsoft's increasingly outdated focus on the desktop and client/server computing. Indeed, Frankenberg articulated a future vision of network-based computing (now called the "Cloud"), but nobody listened, and he failed to get their attention.

Hubris

We think of hubris as inflation arising from overestimated capability. In Greek mythology, hubris often involves an act that intrudes on the domain of the gods. The Greek deities had a keen sense of proportion and would not let any challenge go unpunished. The Greek goddess Nemesis inflicted retribution on anyone who succumbed to hubris. In modern usage, nemesis means something that a person cannot overcome or someone who cannot be defeated, or an act of retribution. Let's see how this unfolds in corporate life.

An example of hubris was 3Com, founded in 1979 based on technology developed at Xerox PARC for connecting computers to a network. Ethernet became a major standard for networking, and 3Com's Ethernet adapters quickly dominated the market. The company had a successful initial public offering (IPO).

Subsequently, in a case of what we might call "anticipated hubris," the company decided to branch out into servers, or computers attached to the network. This move took the company away from its core competence (data networking) and put it into competition with some of its major customers, such as IBM. Building servers is very different from building network adapters, and it was not a company core competence. 3Com also lacked the necessary software for network operations and licensed a network operating system from Microsoft, meaning it no longer had exclusive ownership of its own core intellectual property. It also created an entirely new business with a different marketing strategy and a different organization.

Soon thereafter, 3Com acquired Bridge Communications, a bridge and router provider. Bridges and routers are intermediate systems, between the network adapters at individual devices and the network servers. The Bridge acquisition enabled 3Com to offer a full network solution, a powerful position in the emerging industry. Unfortunately, the company botched the merger, leading one of the

Bridge executives to declare, "We are the division that management performs medical experiments on."

Eventually, after years of investing hundreds of million dollars, the integrated network business initiative failed, and Eric Benhamou, who came to 3Com as part of the Bridge acquisition, took over as CEO. The company then went through a wrenching and expensive transition to shed the server business units, exit the network operating system contract with Microsoft, lay off staff, take a massive charge to earnings, and embark on the process of returning to its network knitting, its core competence, including the beleaguered Bridge router business. After "crossing the desert," as Benhamou later characterized the transition, the downsized 3Com business stabilized, yet some ground was never recaptured. Throughout this period, Cisco, steadfastly sticking to their knitting, rose against only weak opposition from 3Com to its dominating position in the global router market.

Nemesis requires a redemptive act. 3Com paid dearly for its corporate hubris. In many cultures, a redemptive act may involve a sacrifice to the gods. In a modern-day public company, a redemptive act might mean a precipitous drop in stock price.

Illusion

Illusion, "something that deceives by producing a false or misleading impression of reality," is also a common affliction in business. Illusion differs from inflation and hubris. It entails an inability to see things clearly.

A company with roots in a prestigious research organization as part of a large Fortune 100 company was spun out after six years and $10M in research and development. The company then evolved over several years through a series of odd startup maneuvers. By the time the board recruited a new CEO, the spinout had gone through about $30M in investment with little to show for it.

The company was formed in an incubator alongside another startup that provided nearly identical software functionality for a similar market. The other company grew quickly and went public, generating substantial financial rewards for its team members. The first incubator team took a more circuitous path but always believed, as the other company's "lost twin," it would achieve a comparable outcome. This idealized expectation proved to be illusory.

The new CEO, after quickly reducing expenses, consummated a partnership with a leading aircraft company. On the strength of this engagement, the company raised about $10M and converted a $5M bridge loan into equity. The dream of mimicking its "lost twin's" success seemed well on the way to fulfillment.

Unfortunately, the startup firm's second illusion was the belief that the engineering team inherited from the airline partner had the technical capability to build the product. After several months, it became obvious this simply was not the case.

The third illusion concerned the sales cycle. It turned out that the *technical* buyer and the *economic* buyer were separated in the customer organizations. That is, while the technical buyer understood very well the efficiency gains provided by the product, the economic buyer for a purchase of this magnitude was more concerned with controlling expenses. Consequently, the sales cycles were much longer than originally anticipated, and the number of sales also was overestimated.

The fourth illusion was shattered when a serious case of management misbehavior emerged. So much for the illusion of professional and responsible management.

In Hindu mythology, Maya is the goddess of illusion. Maya also appears in Buddhist, Jain, and Sikh traditions. Illusion as a personified figure in the divine pantheon suggests that illusion has an archetypal grip on human life, and therefore on teams. We should anticipate illusion to be a force in play that needs to be respected. For purposes of leadership, Maya does not mean "false" so much as "things are often not as they appear to be."

A long-held belief of mine is that one of the most difficult challenges of leadership is to have the executive team arrive at a common view of reality. Much has been written on this topic. The process of arriving at a common and coherent view can only begin with the presumption of incompleteness. Awareness that we are often automatically drawn into a state of illusion motivates proper attention to the matter, as opposed to relying on the working assumption that things are going well. Hence, once again, the vital question: "What are we not thinking about?" Searching for what we are not thinking about can feel both onerous and unnatural, which it is.

This quest honors the critical eye. Theresa Johnston in "Why Criticism Is Good for Innovation" (*Stanford GSB Magazine*, Spring, 2016) writes about Professor Jonathan Bendor: "Many people believe that criticism and creativity are incompatible in the workplace. But as Bendor sees it, creativity and criticism are like the Chinese principles of Yin and Yang: two complementary forces that interact to form a greater whole. 'I think not only can they live together,' he says, 'they *have* to live together.'" (italics added)

PART IV

Practices

The How of Leadership

CHAPTER 23

COMMUNICATION PRACTICE

The Role of Communication in Team Performance

n this chapter, we discuss the importance of communication in promoting team performance. Here, we find Hermes particularly helpful when we provide suggestions and guidelines for implementing practices tested and proven in multiple organizations. Properly adopted and modeled by the leadership and embraced across the team, the four elements of communication—open, inclusive, direct, truthful—can dramatically improve performance. When built on the foundational principles of empathy, complementarity, and nonattachment, they transform creative collaboration. The self-regulating organization that results is then on a path to continuous collaboration and improvement.

Many leaders subscribe to the notion that "information is power" (a paradigm of Machiavelli), and tend to hoard information versus serving it up to team members. But improving all facets of communication is the quickest step toward a healthier team environment. In fact, communication is *the* essential underlying practice for enabling creative collaboration.

This practice applies to all kinds of organizations, even athletic teams. In "Warriors: Team Building," an article published in the *New York Times* as the Golden State Warriors were on the rise in 2016, Bruce Schoenfeld highlighted some facets of the team's management style. As Schoenfeld explained, "Steve Kerr may not have seemed a likely choice when he was brought in as head coach after the 2014 season. But his open communication style made a difference on many levels. During the 2015 championship series, when the Warriors were 2–1 behind Cleveland, Kerr's assistant, Nick U'Ren, who was responsible for making the music playlists for practices and creating highlight reels, watched a tape of the 2014 playoffs and saw how San Antonio defended LeBron James. U'Ren then "suggested that the Warriors replace Bogut in the lineup with Andre Iguodala, who is half a foot shorter but athletic enough to at least force James to work to get good shots. Kerr took the suggestion, and the Warriors didn't lose another game."

Not only did Kerr take U'Ren's suggestion, he gave him public credit for it. As Shaun Livingston, a Warriors guard who had then played for nine other organizations, told Schoenfeld, "I've never seen anything like that. This wasn't even an assistant coach; it was a video coordinator. And Steve Kerr listened to him, and he did it. All the bridges are open here. There's an open forum of ideas. A good idea really can come from anywhere. And that kind of thinking has to start at the top."

Exactly. We have found time and again that opening all doors and windows has profound effects on the team in terms of productivity and morale. Key suggestions for promoting healthy and productive communication follow; each is elaborated in turn.

- Ensure communication is *open, inclusive, direct, truthful*
- Require that communication be respectful and preserving of dignity

- Resolve conflict quickly
- Drive out indirect communication
- Explain that staying within the confines of the company's operating principles means you cannot get fired (a kind of diplomatic immunity).

OPEN, INCLUSIVE, DIRECT, AND TRUTHFUL COMMUNICATION

What is required for open, inclusive, direct, and truthful communication? There's a lot packed into those four words, much of it related to creating an environment in which everyone feels safe and is engaged.

Open

For communication to be truly open, people must understand that they can speak their minds fully without risk. It also requires that people at all levels feel comfortable speaking, knowing they will not be threatened or punished if they voice concerns. This may take some time, but given the importance of psychological safety, it is indispensable.

Inclusive

Even in an atmosphere of psychological safety, leaders often need to take additional steps to ensure that those who might be hesitant or feel they lack opportunities to speak are included and heard. Individuals who spot problems or have creative ideas do not automatically share their thoughts (whether because of their position or their personality). You need to ensure that communication is encouraged and inclusive. You must increase the likelihood of hearing the "small voice in the room," where creativity is often concealed and awaiting notice. Think of the Warriors case. Sometimes that small voice that can prevent or resolve problems is not even in the room and must be sought out.

For example, Ken Blanchard, author of *The One Minute Manager*, tells the story of a country club board of directors trying to reduce expenses. The directors noticed that the locker room expenses seemed high and had a long debate about how they might reduce them. They identified locker room supplies, especially shampoo, as having spiked recently and suspected certain items were ending up in members' homes. They tried to come up with a method for controlling the leakage but were stumped. Finally, someone had the bright idea of consulting the locker room manager. He listened, and then declared, "No problem. I will take care of it." Curious, the board representative persisted until the locker room manager explained "I'll take the caps off the shampoo bottles." Simple, immediate cost-saving solution. No debate required.

Another example. Missed communication (often due to an environment in which people do not feel safe) can have a dramatic effect on the bottom line.

One promising startup company had entered an agreement with a much larger, high-profile player in the industry. This partnership had the potential to put the startup on the map and create a high valuation for subsequent investment rounds. The company was late delivering a hardware/software card to the partner, but eventually delivered it. The larger partner took three months to begin testing the card, during which further development of the card by the startup was suspended. Once testing began, the card was discovered to be irretrievably flawed, and the partnership collapsed.

During the testing process with the larger partner, one of the startup engineers was heard to say "They *should* be mad. That card is junk!" Had that fact been widely understood, the startup company could have used those three months to fix the card and save the partnership.

Instead, another startup, employing a similar technology strategy, but running months behind, gained traction. It ultimately went public and ultimately was sold for $3 billion. The first startup eventually sold for $50 million, or a difference in outcome of $2.95 billion. That's an expensive communication mishap. Hermes wept.

It may seem obvious, but it's often overlooked: *Someone* on the team always knows there is a problem before it's detected by management. Why wait for a business post mortem to encourage them to share what they know?

Direct

It may seem obvious, but the point is too often missed or ignored. As a team member, you must speak directly with the people who can do something about the problem. That is, those who have the authority to act on the information you can share to the overall benefit of the team.

Truthful

This means telling the truth in its entirety. This does not mean "tell all" as a general principle. There are sometimes topics—such as the details of a strategic negotiating underway, whether there will be a layoff, or individual compensation—that need at least interim privacy. Also, open communication requires team members to keep company information confidential. However, as a general principle, if you want to eliminate secrecy, eliminate secrets and encourage rather than discourage truth telling. This establishes a two-way agreement with the team: I will share information and you will keep it confidential. Although seeking or revealing personal information can be awkward, if critical to the business mission it should not be evaded or post-poned, as the following story illustrates.

Lost in Translation: How Not to Communicate

The lead investor on the board of directors was a genius at spread-sheets, the Mozart of Excel, and could drill any quantitative topic into the ground. At one point, he developed an elaborate formula for sales commissions, involving complex formulas designed to spur the sales force on to greater and greater feats of selling. But the timing was way off: The sales team was attempting to get simple traction, and his formulas speculated in realms of sales volume off in the far future.

Somehow, he always seemed to be off point. Granted, it was a difficult time. The prior CEO, lacking experience, had wasted a great deal of capital pursuing hopeless paths to revenue growth; the investors (who were by then in for over $20M), were nervous because there had been no growth over several years. But this particular investor's skewed focus stood out.

This made communication, well, weird—and the executive team was increasingly frustrated. Concerned that the team might simply rebel and check out, the CEO addressed the lead investor's behavior, privately. In the moment, he seemed less than pleased, and they left the conversation competing for the title of most justifiably alienated. He later invited the CEO out for a beer for a "confession" and explained that he simply could not understand conversations without seeing something explicitly in print. That little piece of information made for an "Aha!" moment: That's why more than a year of communication with him often went nowhere. Had the CEO known, he could have modified his approach to collaborating with him from the beginning; knowing, he then understood why he had missed the boat earlier in the company's history.

This was a communication problem, one of many layers. As both a cognitive and a behavioral problem, it's complicated.

An inability to communicate (and to understand communication without visuals) would have a negative effect on relatedness, and subsequently on communication, collaboration, and ultimately trust. That's the problem.

The other, a meta-problem, was the failure to communicate about the communication problem. What might it have taken for him to reveal this earlier, in confidence? Surely, few of us are comfortable revealing our challenges, but not sharing the information with those who needed to know only made the problems worse. The decision not to share the problem due to embarrassment or other sensitivity dumps the problem on the other parties, who cannot figure out why mutual dialogue is so unproductive. They may wonder if the investor simply discounts the content of presentations and are left feeling that they have been neither seen nor heard. The investor not informing those who were attempting their best to communicate with him was less than productive (and bordered on narcissistic).

His apparent obsessive belief in the power of spreadsheets eventually alienated the entire executive team—and should have been an early clue. A good spreadsheet can catalog and clarify an enormous amount of material, but it can also distract from or stand as a poor substitute for the actual human-to-human encounter. Relatedness simply doesn't fit on a spreadsheet. No surprise then that we have yet to find a company that can be successfully led through the thin straw of Excel.

But differences in communication modalities? Not a problem—once you know. And once you understand the utterly essential need for communication, you also might become more attuned to whether someone prefers visual, auditory, or written styles. If you sense something, ask. And if you have a particular style you prefer, inform your business partners. They need to know how best to communicate with you, and you with them. Having the confidence to share this information will help you all avoid problems later.

FURTHER COMMUNICATION PRACTICES: THE IRREDUCIBLE NEED FOR CONSTANT COMMUNICATION

Finally, leadership must accept the irreducible need for constant communication. It may be impossible to communicate too much. George Bernard Shaw was quoted as saying, "The single biggest problem with communication is the illusion that it has taken place." In one company, the CEO was certain he had adequately communicated his vision for the company, and *nobody* on the executive team agreed with that assessment. When leadership does not provide adequate information, the team will fill in the details with the worst case, sometimes even with bizarre versions of reality.

Respectful Communication

Leadership must also model and require that communication be respectful and preserving of dignity. Communication can be straightforward without devolving into harsh confrontation, the antithesis to the practices that support creative collaboration. In one company, a team member berated another executive in the hallway well within earshot of the entire team. When the CEO confronted him on his behavior, he said he was "just using direct communication," pursuant to their express company value. Because respect was also another company value, the CEO explained that he got an "A" on direct and an "F" on respect and put him on probation. Employees in other companies using "constructive confrontation" as a practice are heard in the hallways to refer to it as "destructive confrontation," due to the lack of an explicit focus on respect as a corollary and equally important value.

Resolve Conflict Quickly

Many leaders avoid conflict or simply delay dealing with it. That can be deadly for two reasons. One is the consequences of the conflict itself, where an unsolved problem festers. For example, a CEO that does not confront a subordinate executive bullying people means team members continue to be bullied. The other meta-reason is that the entire team (excluding the offending executive) loses confidence that the CEO "has their back" and motivation suffers accordingly. Conflict is common, and the higher the pace and energy of the team, the more conflict will happen. Lack of conflict is a flat line on the team heart monitor. The objective is to resolve conflict quickly, as soon as it shows up.

Indirect Communication

Indirect communication—talking about a problem with someone who does not have the power to solve the problem—quickly devolves into "toxic gossip." Gossip can be addictive and, while sometimes emotionally satisfying, it misdirects energy and creates a negative atmosphere. Such gossip can take place not just in face-to-face conversation, but also in email, text, social media, and voicemail. People will learn that they've been talked about behind their backs. No one likes it, and trust can't survive in such an environment.

SAFETY IN PRINCIPLES

Leadership must establish that those who stay within the boundaries of the company's operating principles in their communications cannot get fired. (All the more reason for establishing a strong statement of principles and practices that mirrors what is described in this book.) Think of the process as establishing a kind of diplomatic immunity. Given that the operating principles include delivering on commitments, ensuring safety is *not* a risk, nor does it encourage anarchy or permit nonperformance. Team members who *do* deliver on commitments reliably also enjoy the privilege of protected speech, as long as it remains respectful.

Write It Down

I have found that a written statement of operation principles, posted on the conference room wall, is very helpful in getting increasing compliance. You can invite the entire team to provide edits, and then sign the document as a means of gaining adoption.

CHAPTER 24

CASE STUDY: NASA

Catastrophic Consequences of Poor Communication

F ailure to create an effective culture of communication can not only lead to loss of profit and market share, it can be downright catastrophic. On February 1, 2003, the space shuttle *Columbia*, with seven astronauts on board, ended an expected routine reentry in a flaming breakup that killed all its occupants and scattered 84,000 fragments of the shuttle over hundreds of square miles.

Seventeen years and 89 shuttle missions earlier, the shuttle *Challenger* had ended in an explosive tragedy of similar scale. The real tragedy is that both events might have been avoided had the right communication practices been the established norm in NASA.

The investigation of the *Columbia* incident, following the 2003 explosion, revealed that on multiple occasions the potential of damage to the wing during ascent—which in turn could lead to a catastrophic reentry—was raised by engineers. After *Columbia* reached orbit, a back-channel request was sent to the Department of Defense to use secret military satellites to photograph the shuttle in orbit to determine the extent of the damage, if any, that *Columbia* might have suffered during liftoff. The Air Force would have been glad to oblige, but NASA management withdrew the request later. Low-level engineers also sent their superiors an email query about the possibility of the astronauts conducting a spacewalk, which would have been easily accomplished, to inspect the wing. The email was never answered.

The result of all these missteps was that the damaged wing was not properly assessed, and the *Columbia* crew was sent into a reentry maneuver that was not survivable.

Retired four-star admiral Hal Gehman, assigned to head the *Columbia* Accident Investigation Board, or CAIB, explained the following to William Langewiesche, in an *Atlantic Monthly* article that ran in November 2003 headlined "*Columbia*'s Last Flight":

> They claim that the culture in Houston is a "badge-less society," meaning it doesn't matter what [title] you have on your badge—you're concerned about shuttle safety [just like everyone else]. Well, that's all nice, but the truth is that it *does* matter what badge you're wearing.
>
> Look, if you really do have an organization that has free communication and open doors and all that kind of stuff, *it takes a special kind of management to make it work* [italics added]. And we just don't see that management here.
>
> Oh, they *say* all the right things ... but then when you look at how it really works, it's an incestuous, hierarchical system, with invisible rankings and a very strict informal chain of command. They all know that. So even though they've got all the trappings of communication, you don't actually *find* communication. We have plenty of witness statements saying, "If I had spoken up, it would have been at the cost of my job."

Not only was there no real support for open communication, the management acted in a way that actually discouraged it. One of the decision-makers most closely associated with *Columbia*'s final flight, and the leader of the post-flight Mishap Investigation Team, was "an intimidating figure" … "known for a tough and domineering management style. Among the lower ranks she had a reputation for brooking no nonsense and being a little hard to talk to. She was not smooth. … She was said to have a difficult personality," NASA employees told the *Atlantic Monthly*.

The following exchange tells you all you need to know about her style. One of CAIB's investigators asked her, "As a manager, how do you seek out dissenting opinions?"

"Well, when I hear about them …"

"By their very nature you may not hear about them," he replied.

"Well, when someone comes forward and tells me about them," she carried on …

"But what techniques do you use to *get* them?"

She apparently had no answer.

In a later interview in *Stanford Magazine*, Douglas Osheroff, a Nobel Laureate in physics and a member of the Columbia Accident Investigation Board, connected the same root cause to the earlier *Challenger* disaster. "(W)hen some of the engineers tried to figure out exactly how bad the damage was, they were rebuffed. If you look at the emails and correspondence that took place … it sort of reminds you of the *Challenger* disaster. I mean, structurally the two events were very different. But this business about NASA not listening to its engineers was similar in both cases. The managers at NASA were willing to accept a risk that they did not understand at all."

Later in the same interview, Osheroff gets really close to the main issue. "I wanted a [board] recommendation that said NASA's culture has to change. The board in general felt that we had made a very compelling case and NASA had to recognize this, but that we couldn't tell them *how* to change their culture."

This book tells you how you actually *can* change the culture of your team.

NASA is an example of leadership that focused on the wrong task. They were concerned about creating a compliant bureaucracy rather than a team effectively executing its mission. By suppressing dissent and the expression of team creativity, much was sacrificed, including the lives of astronauts.

Our claim is not that leadership is not necessary. That would be absurd. It is that leadership needs to understand how to improve communication. And this is less obvious than it may appear.

CULTIVATING WISDOM WITH MYTH

Imagine being steeped in the wisdom of the ages distilled in fables, fairy tales, and myths as children and adolescents. How might ancient myths help us address the issues of adulthood and career in our times?

. . .

G. Kwame Scruggs imagined the possibilities. Through his organization, Alchemy, Inc., he has used myths to great effect with over 1,500 male youths since 2003, 95% of whom are from urban neighborhoods in Akron or Cleveland. Most of them are African-American. They face challenges of apathy, anger, drugs, violence, and victimhood.

Before starting Alchemy, Kwame worked at Goodyear in Akron, Ohio, for 15 years. During those years, he attended night school to earn his bachelor's degree. He obtained his master's degree at the University of Akron, and worked at the university while completing a second master's degree in Community Counseling. There, Kwame encountered the works of Carl Jung and Joseph Campbell. Seized by Campbell's admonition to "follow your bliss," Kwame decided to do just that. After receiving an MA and a Ph.D. in Mythological Studies (with an emphasis on Jungian Depth Psychology) from the Pacifica Graduate Institute in 2009, he formed Alchemy as a nonprofit organization to "assist urban adolescent males to develop a sense of purpose in life and successfully function as members of a family, school, and community."

Alchemy uses myths to help students develop critical thinking skills and constructive behavior. Dozens of myths and open-ended questions provoke dialogue about life's great issues—all while creating a supportive community with shared knowledge and common goals. Kwame relates old tales and myths to the rhythm of a compelling beat, taking breaks for questions about narrative events and mythic imagery in each story. These questions launch discussions about the meaning embedded in the stories, possible parallels in the students' lives, and the issues they face. Kwame helps his students perceive and consider recurring mythical themes that shed light on their personal circumstances.

As one example, Kwame uses *The Water of Life*, a German fairy tale collected by the Brothers Grimm. The script for Kwame's retelling of the tale runs 18 pages, interspersed with multiple exercises and 24 multiple question sets. The questions do more than keep the students engaged. As the following excerpts demonstrate, they also reinforce the links between an ancient story and modern-day life:

> Once upon a time—long, long ago—there once was a king who was sick, and no one thought he would live. **And when the king is sick, the entire village is sick.** He had three sons who were very sad. They went down to the palace garden and wept. An old man came by and asked them why they were weeping. They told him their father was sick and sure to die, for nothing seemed to cure him, nothing did him any good. The old man said, "I know of one more remedy: the Water of Life. If he drinks of that, he'll get well, but it's hard to find."

> *Questions: What does it mean that "when the king is sick, the entire village is sick"? What or who is the "king" in your life right now? Is that king well or sick?*

> The sons beg the king to let them go on a journey to seek the water of life. The first son goes off and abuses a dwarf along the way. The abused dwarf wreaks revenge on that son. The second son repeats the mistake and suffers the consequences. The third son befriends the dwarf, who then provides him with critical information in his quest for the Water of Life.

> *Questions:* What was the difference in the three brothers? What have you "dwarfed" in your life?

The dwarf warns the third son about lions appearing on the path. The son feeds them bread provided by the dwarf to distract them and escape.

Question: Feeding the lions is like feeding something that can be devouring—i.e., a drug habit, a gambling habit, a drinking habit. Are there any "lions" you are presently feeding?

Much later, the youngest son was betrayed by his older two brothers.

Questions: Betrayal is a common theme in myth. Chances are, it is a common theme in life. Reflect back on a time when you were betrayed by someone close to you. Reflect on a time that you might have betrayed someone close to you. *Write down a few thoughts on how you felt and possibly still feel.*

Alchemy's website (http://alchemyinc.net) cites the Hasidic proverb "Give people a fact or an idea and you enlighten their minds; tell them a story and you touch their souls." It also explains that "We are more about cultivating wisdom than teaching knowledge."

And the students clearly get it. Just a few of the testimonials provide a glimpse of how deeply the program has affected them.

As weeks went on, I noticed a change in myself. I was studying more, working harder in sports, and acting more and more like an adult. … I was a raw element being changed into something beautiful and new. I was looking forward to something new to experience every day.

There was a change in my home life. My mom no longer had to tell me to clean my room or do chores. I simply did them. Relationships also seemed to change significantly. I found myself judging people less and less. … I was being open to let people know me. The biggest change of all was that I learned, in any aspect of life, you get out what you put in. This means that you cannot put in 50% effort and expect 100% results.

The more I stayed in the group, the more college seemed like the for sure next step in my future.

One student said the program was like "having a parent with you all the time." Of the myths, others said, "They are easy to understand, they are interesting, they make you think" and "even though they are not true, they can help you in everyday life." Another student acknowledged that myths enable you to learn from others' mistakes, as well as from what people in the myths did to help others and themselves.

These students obviously knew the myths were not true. It didn't matter. They knew they contained truth that could be applied to their lives and help them make the transition from boyhood to adulthood.

Alchemy's website gives further testimonials and impressive details about participants' improved involvement in academics and in their communities. Of the first core group of 24, 16 have either graduated or are in school. Several are already in graduate school or have received master's degrees. Younger participants number 54, and the plan is to keep them in the program until they graduate from high school.

Kwame has been widely recognized for his pioneering work. He accepted a National Arts and Humanities Youth Program Award from First Lady Michelle Obama at the White House on November 19, 2012, for his work using myths and drumming to empower urban youth.

CHAPTER 25

COMMITMENT PRACTICE

Real versus False Commitments

This chapter summarizes the commitment practice my co-author and I described nearly two decades ago, augmenting that practice with real-world experiences gained since that time. I also include a number of mini case studies illustrating the importance of effective commitment, often by cataloging the egregious consequences of breaching that practice.

Commitment is not an act, nor a guarantee of a specific outcome. It is an intention with no conditions. It is an internal state of mind without hidden reservations, qualifications, or provisions. It means that if you say you will meet at noon for lunch, you intend to meet at lunch and will manage to arrive there on time. That commitment doesn't include an unspoken proviso saying you'll meet at noon—unless something else pops up. It also doesn't mean you will guarantee being there at noon, given that accidents and other insurmountable obstacles can happen.

Yet, as we all know, managing commitments can be a tricky matter, and many teams routinely suffer failed commitments. Here, we explore why and how we can guard against it. If, for instance, something goes wrong that is outside of a team member's control, we might:

- Remind him or her that failure to meet commitments leads to drama in the organization
- Allow time to consider commitment
- Focus on internal commitments first, at the expense of external commitments
- Renegotiate commitments as necessary when an original commitment becomes impossible to meet

FALSE COMMITMENTS LEAD TO DRAMA

Commitment as a state of mind, and not an externally verifiable fact, raises some problems (and accounts for much of the drama in the world). For how do you know that a spoken commitment flows from a true intent to deliver, when the intent itself is not an observable fact? How do you know whether a commitment can be relied on?

False commitment is saying "yes" when not really meaning it. Take a moment to think about when you made a false commitment or were the party hurt by someone making a false commitment to you. Walk through the process in your mind from beginning to end. What happened?

Chances are there was a significant reaction, also known as gratuitous drama. In teamwork, gratuitous drama leads to at least two problems:

1. We need to figure out how to complete the intended task despite the failed commitment. If team members took enough time to set up the task in the first place, presumably it was sufficiently important to consider other paths to completion. What are they?
2. Then there's the usual meta-worry: Can we rely on each other? Are we a second-rate organization? Should I be spending my time here or somewhere else?

Further, commitments create an asymmetric exchange. Once a commitment is made, the team (or individual) relies on its execution for the common good. As a result, commitments create a kind of dependency that is not under the control of the person or the team to which the commitment has been made. At the same time, those making the commitment may be oblivious of, or indifferent to, that dependency. They may simply decide something more important came up, agreed to it in the first place with unexpressed mental reservations, or simply don't care very much about how failure to meet that commitment affects other team members. This sets the stage for frustration, disappointment, and anger.

All the more reason to consider commitments carefully, in advance.

TAKE THE TIME TO CONSIDER COMMITMENT

Authentic commitments begin when made. Address any doubts up front ("Honor doubt"). A culture in which saying "No" is discouraged or a culture of forced commitments (often disguised as "gung ho") can be disastrous. Allowing forced commitments as an organizational habit means leadership prefers happy talk to results. Further, sweeping doubts under the rug simply postpones the eventual encounter with reality. Conversely, as Jung points out, facing doubt up front yields benefits: "Wherever belief reigns, doubt lurks in the background. But thinking people welcome doubt: it serves them as a valuable stepping stone to better knowledge."

FOCUS ON QUALITY

Internally, false commitments have a serious effect on team morale and energy. If false commitments go unaddressed, team members assume that leadership doesn't care, so why should they? But people *do* care. So now they are in a no-win situation. If they continue to contribute energetically, they may be concerned it will be wasted effort.

In addition, what happens in the core team radiates to the entire team, and from there out to customers, suppliers, investors, and other shareholders. The quality of your commitments to customers is limited to the quality of commitments made internally. Sales, for example, depends on engineering to deliver on products, adhering to the schedule promised to the customer. Communication about product status, customer support, and company direction is critical to forming a durable bond with customers. Just as the CEO's capabilities place a ceiling on how far the culture can evolve, the culture places a ceiling on the quality of its external commitments.

RENEGOTIATE COMMITMENTS AS NECESSARY

Leadership needs to proactively deal with schedule slippages, because allowing them to go unaddressed sends a terrible message to the overall team. There are three choices to consider:

1. Recommit to the original commitment and stay on track. In the weekly project team meeting, when something is behind schedule, the question is "How do we work around the problem?" That is, the default mode is not to accept the consequences of the problem, but to fight back hard against its impact on performance. This increases the likelihood of finding a solution and communicates an overall intolerance for poor performance. It also may put additional pressure on making careful commitments in the first place.
2. Change the timeline or resource. If the first option doesn't produce a solution, the cycle goes back to the beginning with a revised commitment and implementation plan.
3. Remove the owner of the endangered commitment from the delivery process. This sends a strong message but may also be disruptive to team morale. However, if the first two options fail, this action is probably necessary.

IMPORTANCE OF AUTHENTIC COMMITMENT TO EXECUTION: COMMITMENT AND BETRAYAL

Getting commitments right is critical to establishing *Blueprint.* Indeed, Daniel Prosser's book *Thirteeners* promotes the kind of open, collaborative system we are discussing here and suggests that leaders' primary responsibility is to manage commitments more than simply holding people accountable. Still, unfulfilled commitments remain common.

One persistent instance of unfulfilled commitments and gratuitous drama involves the (often troubled) relationship between startup CEOs and the board of directors, which typically is dominated by investors. CEOs commit to deliver specified results (revenue growth, profitability, "burn rate," key milestones, etc.) and the investors commit to continue to fund the company contingent on acceptable performance. In one instance, a new CEO was brought in to a stalled company, and the CEO negotiated in January a commitment from the investors that they would fund the company with an additional round in June, contingent on meeting certain objectives. The CEO did his part, securing new customers and executing a layoff in early June to bring spending in line with objectives. When it came time for the investors to honor their funding commitment, however, one balked, and decided to pull out. The CEO had to implement a second layoff only a couple weeks after the first, with devastating effects on team morale and board credibility. The company continued on a starvation diet for six months, made further progress, and eventually was acquired. However, had the funding commitment been met, it could have secured a much better outcome.

We have witnessed multiple cases of failed investor commitments. It seems as if the prevalent mindset among investors often is that their side of the commitment relationship has carte blanche to be free to take any action favorable to them, and that there is no "meta-commitment" to honor commitments. On the other hand, there are countless examples in high-tech startups where the company failed to meet its commitments to investors. In that case, drama can elevate to a common denouement: loss of additional funding and the end of the company.

Unfulfilled commitments result in demoralized teams and deprive an organization of the enthusiasm, energy, and dedication that investors presumably want to accompany the use of their capital. James Hillman provides a useful characterization of how failures to meet critical commitments engender a sense of betrayal and reviews the dangers that provokes. The first of these dangers is *revenge*: "An eye for an eye; evil for evil; pain for pain." Concerning the preceding examples, of course the (legal) opportunities for revenge against a board of directors are limited. But loss of passion and diminished productivity are almost unavoidable. Less bang for the investor buck. The second danger is *denial*: When we are let down by someone, we are tempted to deny their value, and mostly the company or cause, perhaps thinking "I never thought this was going anywhere anyway." One feels the collapse of hopes and expectations altogether. Something important in us packs up and moves out. The third danger is *cynicism*: "From broken idealism is patched together a tough philosophy of cynicism." A final danger is *self-betrayal*: "My ambitions to make a difference and change the world are sentimental nonsense, a laughable dream now seen as ridiculous." This corrosive effect on our most deeply held values is probably the biggest danger of all.

It is also helpful to remember there is a certain asymmetry here. As Dennis Prager said in *The Rational Bible*: "Human beings tend to much more quickly forget the good others have done for them than the bad others have done to them."

CHAPTER 26

CLOSURE PRACTICE

A Neglected Practice

Closure is the "date" part of an agreement. That is: Closure = Commitment + Date. It provides certainty about the timing of the next action. Neglecting the date part of an agreement is so often the cause of poor performance and unnecessary drama that it needs special focus. Yet, given its powerful effect on execution, there is surprisingly little analysis of how to achieve closure in business literature.

Suggestions for instituting closure include the following, which are covered in more detail in this section:

- Recognizing the consequences of non-closure
- Developing a culture of closure
- Making it visible

RECOGNIZING THE CONSEQUENCES
OF NON-CLOSURE

To illustrate the importance of closure, consider a simple example. You are at work and your mechanic calls to say that your car maintenance will unfortunately not be completed by the end of the day and he will need to keep your car overnight. Oh, great. You were expecting to drive it home that night. Then you see Frank, who lives in your neighborhood, and you ask if you can bum a ride home. Frank disappears. So, you start wondering. Did Frank hear me? Is he offended because I asked him for the favor? Can he not give me a ride? What time would he leave work? Has he forgotten that I gave him a ride to the airport last month? I like Frank, but is he just selfish? His kids seem like brats, so maybe he's a bad parent, too? And on and on. Notice the descent to the *ad hominem* argument ("the fallacy of attacking an opponent's character rather than answering his argument"), the lowest form of rhetoric, used out of desperation.

What's the point? Simply put, lack of closure leads to wondering. The greater the concern for the matter ("How will I get home tonight?" or "Will the investor send the funds before payroll is due?"), the greater the worry. And wondering is the breeding ground of suspicion. This unresolved suspicion then leads to mistrust, and mistrust writ large leads to a disastrous culture of low performance. So, closure is critical to trust and to execution.

We see non-closure when someone says, "I will take care of it" or "I will follow up." Often, the person is acting with goodwill, but simply has not internalized the task enough to accurately forecast the completion date. The intent may be generous or be done simply to appear to "go along with the program." Either may sound good, but what we want is a commitment to follow through by a specific date.

Closure makes for good meetings. In one case, a CEO would spend the entire two-hour weekly staff meeting pontificating about her management philosophy and general view of life…and then adjourn the meeting. There was no closure. So, there was nothing accomplished, and nothing frustrates high-performance executives like inaction and wasted time.

During her absence while on vacation, a consultant took over the meeting and went right to the major issues of the day, discussed possibilities, defined tasks and owners, and established due dates. Enthusiasm went through the roof and the place came alive with creativity. Later, one executive described the experience as "the week that was." Unfortunately, the CEO returned and continued her typical staff-meeting behavior. Within a couple months, the team finally rebelled and forced the board to have her fired.

DEVELOPING A CULTURE OF CLOSURE: EVERYBODY'S RESPONSIBILITY

A culture of closure includes the explicit goal that 100% of consequential communication (communication on topics having an effect on performance) is *closed*—that is, it includes a completion date. Where closure communication has not been the standard mode, initiating it may seem a bit awkward at first. People may ask, "Oh, you also want a date?" The answer is "Yes." Once closure becomes everybody's responsibility, dates are offered voluntarily as part of ongoing communication. (This is infinitely preferable to the pervasive habit of waiting to be bludgeoned into providing one.) One implicit closure practice to institute is the 24-Hour Rule, by which we commit in advance to a one-day limit for returning communication. The 24-Hour Rule doesn't mean you have to resolve the issue or have a long communication in return. It means you acknowledge the request to avoid leaving the other person in the dark. You might say "I got your message, but I'm a bit tied up right now and can't talk. Please call me back next week." Closed.

When introducing the practice of closure, you will encounter some resistance, even in the most collegial of teams. Initially, the request for a date may be perceived as a challenge to one's honor; management may feel reluctant to press the matter for the same reason. This means buying into the false notion that asking for a date is tantamount to challenging credibility. Don't buy it. Management's role is to ensure accountability. Keep in mind that inspection is critical to performance. Avoid asking for dates and you provide permission (perhaps unconsciously) to escape accountability; you've then enabled low performance. Tasks that aren't closed don't get done, so getting that date can be one of the most effective methods for driving execution. Further, establishing a track record for execution against schedule provides a highly useful method for assessing overall job performance.

Another example: A company with no culture of closure held an all-day management meeting with its top dozen executives. During the meeting, they talked about all manner of issues and, appropriately, made an action item list with owners and due dates. This sounds good, but for two big problems:

1. A clear-eyed review of dates showed them to be overly optimistic.
2. There was no built-in follow-up. Where there eventually was follow-up, serious slippage or non-performance was apparent.

So, what was the impact? A full day of key executive time taken away from functional roles with no progress on key issues. The universally frustrating experience of meetings without closure: time and money out the door. And then the meta-problem: a sense that we cannot implement, a sense of being stuck and experiencing the lost joy of real achievement.

In contrast, closure provides us with an answer to an ambiguous situation. It allows us to "park" the matter and come back later. "When will you have the next draft of the corporate presentation done?" "Tuesday." Once you have a reliable culture of closure, you can rely on that answer and not worry about the issue until next Tuesday. No need to wonder or worry in the meantime.

Non-closure need not be viewed as a symptom of an irremediable culture. A more accurate characterization is to view it as an *organizational habit* that can be hard to break. Mark Twain's advice applies here: "Habit is habit, and not to be flung out of the window by any man, but coaxed down-stairs one step at a time." Once the importance of closure is explained to team members, and reinforced at every opportunity, you will start seeing incremental improvements. While in a conversation, one party may not offer a date, but the other may request it, which serves as a reminder. Focusing on date accountability in team meetings will move closure toward center-stage as a team practice.

The strongest resistance to introducing closure practice is actually the most legitimate: I can't give you a date because I don't know what it is yet. The solution is the very useful date-for-a-date: "When will you know when the task will be completed? "Well, I can research the matter and give you a date by next Wednesday." Wednesday becomes a date-for-a-date ("D4D" on the action item list). Closure is reached and, again, you can "park" the matter for now.

While the benefits of closure often lead to immediate converts, some parties may resist. One chief technology officer refused to provide a date for product completion on the basis that "I won't know until it *is* done." If you can't take an action until something has happened, nothing *will* happen.

MAKING IT VISIBLE

Write it down. One CEO of my acquaintance didn't write down action items. "I just hire professionals who are responsible and will deliver, so I don't need to check on things." First, as is often repeated, people don't do what you *expect*, they do what you *inspect*. Also, professionals are people, and people sometimes forget, delay, resist, stall, procrastinate, dawdle, blunder, fail, bungle, or dillydally.

How best to track closure? Consider these two useful tools:

1. An action item list with task descriptions, date assigned, target completion date, revised date (in case of subsequent slippage), and general comments.
2. An extended action item list with the preceding information *and* a column for each future week and what the forecasted completion date was for that week.

Imagine that at one meeting the task was forecasted for completion several weeks out on the 15th. A week later, the same task was forecasted for the 22nd, a slip of a week in a week. You then have an instant side-by-side comparison that discloses the slippage. The entire team can see the performance issue, and the responsible person is subject to social exposure without the manager even making an explicit complaint.

When you assemble a team and begin to implement commitment and closure, two processes begin. First, the team happily gives dates for tasks. Then, over the course of several weeks, these dates prove to be optimistic. What follows is an uncomfortable (and sometimes painful) confrontation with reality. With that taste of reality, better forecasts result.

Closure is also a cure for the classic Them-vs.-Us problem. This is a spontaneous phenomenon occurring between groups separated along some dimension, such as physical distance (e.g., different offices or even floors) or different function (e.g., marketing versus engineering, or human resources versus everybody). In one company that was formed through four different acquisitions, there were seven different locations. And, probably more importantly, each of five different C-level executives (CEO, CFO, CMO, CTO, CSO—Chief Sales Officer) was in a different office. Gossip, backstabbing, blaming, and intrigue flourished.

We mentioned psychological safety as the first rule from Google's five keys to a successful team. We can now see that commitment practice addresses the second rule—Dependability: "Can we count on each other to do high-quality work on time?" Closure practice addresses the third rule—Structure and clarity: "Are goals, roles, and implementation plans on our team clear?" Let's now see how our collaboration practice addresses the fourth and fifth rules: Meaning of Work—"Are we working on something that is personally important for each of us?" and Impact of Work—"Do we fundamentally believe that the work we are doing matters?"

CHAPTER 27

CULTURAL FABRIC

How Principles Support Effective Cultural Practices

Perhaps you're wondering how the principles described earlier relate to the practices just presented. The following diagram in Figure 27-1 details some of the key dependencies of effective practice on established principles. We refer to that relationship as forming the "Cultural Fabric." This diagram explains the particular manner in which each principle supports each practice.

We see from this diagram that empathy is critical in all four practices: complementarity assists dialogue, and nonattachment enables creativity.

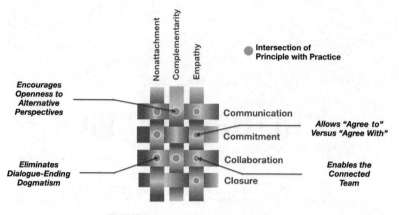

FIGURE 27-1 The Cultural Fabric

CHAPTER 28

TOWARD CULTURAL TRANSFORMATION

A Sealed Container Eliminates Leakage and Loss

I t is often said that changing the culture of an organization is difficult. It is. However, having now reviewed the four practices geared toward execution and high levels of creative collaboration, we can now see how to make that transformation actually happen. In particular, using these practices minimizes what we refer to as "leakage." Leakage, like "drama" or "friction," refers to emotional and behavioral patterns that detract from the pursuit of the mission. Examples of leakage include unexpected slippage in schedules, communication gaps, toxic gossip, inconclusive dialogue, malicious pseudo-compliance, passive-aggressive behavior, betrayal, and widespread disengagement. Collectively, leakage impedes progress and can degrade performance without even being recognized. ("Business as usual, as always.")

The four practices are designed to minimize leakage and acting out. Poor implementation, recidivism, or lack of commitment to using and following through with them enables residual dysfunction, as illustrated in Figure 28-1.

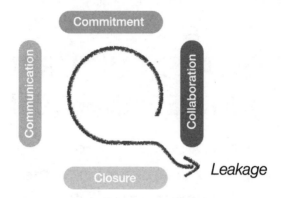

FIGURE 28-1   Incomplete Implementation of the Practices Leads to Leakage

By contrast, complete and consistent implementation prevents leakage and creates a sealed container, within which issues are addressed and resolved as a matter of course, as illustrated in Figure 28-2. Further, a sealed container is effectively self-correcting: Issues are identified, discussed, resolved, and implemented without the constant, and often meddling, oversight of management.

FIGURE 28-2   The Closed Container Supports Continuous Resolution

Alchemy, a proto-scientific method dating back millennia, attempted to convert lead into gold, and entailed a series of steps to achieve that goal. Specifically, the transformative process required a sealed container to progress through the transformation of base elements into something more valuable. It was later understood that alchemy was not real chemistry, but rather a projection of psychological factors onto matter, suggesting that certain human processes must be contained to progress.* Similarly, with the metaphor of a sealed container, we have a crucible in which the practices of communication, collaboration, commitment, and closure enable the evolution of high-performance teams.

---

* C.G. Jung, *Psychology and Alchemy, Collected Works of C. G. Jung*, Volume 12, Princeton, N.J.: Princeton University Press, 1968.

CHAPTER 29

THE SELF-REGULATING ORGANIZATION

Evolution and Radiation

The sealed container leads to the self-regulating organization. This proceeds as follows. At all levels in the organization, team members may observe and report a problem or opportunity, which in turn generates an idea or suggestion. Direct communication (i.e., with the appropriate people) then leads to an instance of creative collaboration, resulting in an agreement. Closure and authentic commitment then follow, providing the assurance of full intent to implement the commitment. The cycle repeats itself—over and over, as well as in parallel at all levels of the organization. Regulation becomes an organic process, versus the need for escalation and top-down direction in the hierarchical organization.

I have always encouraged team members to "Lead from your position." Leadership opportunities are available to everyone, whether it is innovating a new approach to your function, achieving a new level of performance, helping your colleagues, or just speaking up. The underlying idea is that creative action is always possible at all levels in the company, and encouraging it facilitates successful outcomes.

THE RADIATION EFFECT

Let's now look beyond the core team and examine how teamwork influences the external world. What happens in the core team inexorably radiates outward. On the one hand, you cannot honor commitments to customers more than you can honor commitments internally. We have seen many instances where ineffective leadership establishes a low ceiling for the entire team. On the other hand, strong implementation practices in the core team radiate outward across the team and eventually to the customer. As this process is established, it goes through a transformation like that illustrated in the following.

The fluid, agile function of today's business organization resembles a network, a series of nodes more than a hierarchy. Some nodes are larger than others, having more responsibility or a greater skill set. We start with a picture that looks like Figure 29-1.

FIGURE 29-1   Today's Organization: More Network Than Hierarchy

Dysfunctional organizations evolve haphazardly, as illustrated next by what we might call the Random Organization. There are a few strong links (buddies) and a variety of weak, conflicted, or simply missing links, as seen in Figure 29-2.

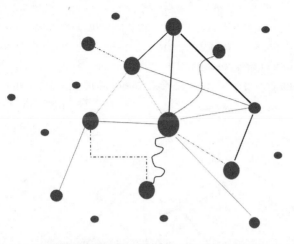

FIGURE 29-2   The Random Organization

Next, if the operating principles and practices we have discussed are adopted and successfully implemented, strong links are formed among members of the core team, as Figure 29-3 shows.

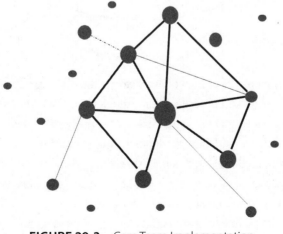

FIGURE 29-3   Core Team Implementation

As this process proceeds out and downward through the organization, it is useful to remember that a manager is not off the hook when they have competent and engaged subordinates—not until their subordinates themselves have competent and engaged subordinates.

Through a training program, formally or with on-the-job coaching, linkages radiate across the organization. This network, the highly connected team, continues to radiate outward into the external world of customers, suppliers, and shareholders, as Figure 29-4 shows.

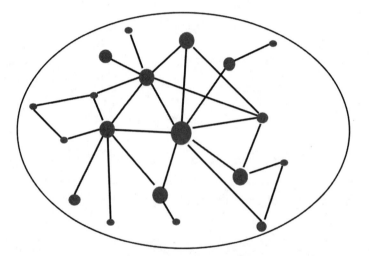

FIGURE 29-4. A New Entity: The Highly Connected Team

The ancients, looking for ways to view and connect to the vast unknown, projected their gods and myths onto the stars in the heavens. In connecting them (and connecting *to* them), they established ways to navigate and find guidance through life, such as connecting through storytelling—with each other, the gods, and the universe.

Today, we don't view the night sky in the same way. Nor do we tell the same stories. Yet the need for connection lives on. The radiation effect shows how connected we are, in ways known, unknown, and hidden. How much more effective could we be if we recognized, understood, and aligned ourselves with that? Creative collaboration enables us to connect the dots in a multitude of ways that can draw from everyone's strengths and continuously readjust organizational priorities and functions to focus on the most appropriate tasks. Open and highly connected networks offer new possibilities for effective teamwork and a self-regulating functionality foreign to top-down hierarchical organizations.

The connected has a beginning, as did the universe, and radiates outward in an analogous manner. What the team is at its core, for better or worse, will radiate out through the organization and beyond. Modern physics tells us that in order to understand the observed behavior of the universe, it is necessary to postulate the existence of "dark matter" and "dark energy." In fact, visible matter is only 15% of the mass of the universe. Dark matter and dark energy constitute the other 85%. Likewise, hidden factors influence every organization. Schedule slippage, gossip, conspiracies, hidden agendas, gratuitous drama, and malicious compliance are indeed hidden "dark" matters.

On the other hand, every organization's constellation of network nodes is a unique pattern replicated nowhere else. There is no other team like this one, and it has its own unique story, or myth, embodying its own meaning. This reminds us of the admonition of William Ouchi, management professor and author, to seek competitive advantages that are difficult to copy. Your highly connected team is both a powerful competitive advantage and difficult to copy.

DRAMA AND DIONYSUS

Understanding Drama in Team Life

One of the recurring themes in this book is drama. Drama is a constant reality in team life. The types of dysfunctional behavior described earlier activate a whole spectrum of emotional responses—fear, resentment, anger, depression—that can all be described as varied species of drama. As we have seen, false commitments, toxic gossip, disrespectful communication—they all generate drama. From the perspective of team performance and execution, drama can be considered the sand in the wheels, the fly in the ointment, the pooper in the party.

But whence drama? Why are people drawn to drama? Is it fuel for their engines, their energy supply, or just a form of entertainment, a welcome diversion from the task at hand? For an answer, we can once again consult the mythic later. Again, we will find a figure with both positive and negative aspects, which means, when we understand mythic figures as embodiments of our basic humanity, we will find those same positive and negative aspects in those humans in our teams. Then with clarity of perception, we can anticipate, observe, diagnose, and prepare for their entrance, and hopefully minimize their negative manifestations while maximizing their positive contributions.

Here, we go back to find the origin of drama in one of the most notorious figures in Greek mythology: Dionysus. He was the god of fertility and wine and spread the art of viniculture. For our purposes, he was also patron god of the Greek stage—the god of drama. He brought joy and divine ecstasy, along with brutal and blinding rage. As such, he was another archetypal figure embodying complementary aspects.

. . .

Dionysus was the son of Zeus. It happened that one day Zeus was tootling around Thebes in Greece. He was going about incognito because mortals could not look at him undisguised lest they perish. He ran across Semele, the daughter of King Cadmus, and fell hopelessly in love—a repetitive inclination for Zeus that was apparently wired into his divine DNA. She reciprocated, and after a few divine frolics became pregnant. At this point, Semele grew desperate to look into the true eyes of her lover—a not unreasonable impulse for a mortal, but a really bad idea when dallying with a god. In a fit of passion, Zeus promised her one wish, swearing on the river Styx (apparently the precursor to "a stack of bibles"). When he heard her wish to see him as he really was, he was gobsmacked. He knew what would happen. He pleaded. She insisted. When he relented and revealed himself in his full glory, she was nearly completely incinerated. The autopsy revealed that only Dionysus, in his first stroke of good luck, survived wrapped in her womb. Zeus then made an incision in his thigh and sewed the infant in it, an obstetric procedure now out of fashion. Zeus then carried Dionysus to term, thereby conferring upon him immortality.

Hera, goddess of jealousy, learning that Dionysus was alive, felt enough was enough. So, she arranged for the Titans, descendants of the first generation of divine beings, to kill Dionysus. The Titans ripped him to pieces and boiled him for good measure. The Mafia would have been impressed. However, the goddess Rhea brought Dionysus back to life. In this way, he was born three times: once from his mother's womb, once from his father's thigh, and once again from the earth under a pomegranate tree. With such a start in life, it seemed Dionysus was destined to be a very unusual member of the Greek pantheon.

Dionysus indeed turned out to be a complex figure. Unlike other gods who kept a constant manifestation, Dionysus could change shape at will: stag, panther, man, goat, god. Cursed by Hera with madness, he traveled the world spreading his art of winemaking and worship. He was known for wild and joyous celebration, inspiring divine ecstasy in the willing, and madness in the opposed. He was the antithesis of law and order. He emblemized the power of his wine to inspire both joy and desperation.

Unfortunately, Dionysus has gotten a bad rap down through the ages. Perhaps some of this is due to confusing him with the god Bacchus, allegedly the Roman version of Dionysus. Dionysus was the god of ecstasy. Bacchus was the god of drunkenness. In fact, Dionysus himself got drunk only once and he didn't like it. One story is that Dionysus turned into a donkey and arrived at Zeus's shrine braying, which became human speech. So, when we get drunk enough to get this jackass aspect going, we are no longer candidates for ecstasy. Our humanness is lost.

Dionysus is therefore the archetype of the basic human drive for ecstasy and joy. His wide-ranging nature set the stage for elaborate treatment in Greek drama.

So that begins to answer our questions. Drama *is* energy, *and* entertainment, *and* distraction. The leadership question, however, is: "Does this lead to *joy* or *desperation*?" Our concern for drama in the team is associated with the latter effect, which we elaborate on throughout this chapter. But what about joy and ecstasy? This prompts a response similar to the hostess who replied to Richard Feynman's request for both milk and lemon in his tea with "Surely you're joking, Mr. Feynman!" Find joy in work with all of its boredom, tedium, suppression, anxiety, and exhaustion? Surely not.

But we think "yes." So, let us count some ways:

- **Integrity.** We mentioned in Chapter 16 that the benefit of living in integrity is joy, and the control signal is anxiety. My experience is that I am much happier when I have stayed on track than when I have screwed things up, based on an impressive amount of anecdotal evidence. A simple example is the 24-Hour Rule mentioned earlier. The idea is that you get back to a communication within 24 hours, even if only to say you cannot communicate now. Closure. This is such a deeply engrained habit of mind for me now that I feel very uncomfortable if I go beyond the time limit. Simple but palpable.

- **Contribution.** We know when we have made a contribution, helped someone, provided a key input, resolved a problem. This involves an inner sense of lifted spirits.
- **Recognition.** We remember recognize means "see again." We were already aware of our own value. Now, with others knowing, that elevates us further.
- **Achievement.** Going further, there is an exuberant moment when, individually or with a team, some accomplishment has been made. This may be completing a project, winning a contract, completing financing, or some other Eureka moment portending great progress. We often even describe ourselves as "ecstatic" when a significant accomplishment has been made.
- **Transcendence.** One of our basic needs is to be part of something bigger than ourselves, which is also the yearning for the ecstatic experience. It seems that this getting out of our own skin and joining with something bigger and more important relates to the yearning for a Dionysian moment.

So, yes, the urge for, and possibility of, joy—and even ecstasy—remains with us today.

Unfortunately, we might have lost the ability to experience the transformative power of ecstasy and joy. Our rational mindset believes that the only thing of value resides in the material realm. This leads to the main problem of our time: addiction. Robert Johnson in *Ecstasy* catalogs the misdirected way that we seek ecstasy: "The successful young entrepreneurs who think they need cocaine to give them the competitive edge; the supermoms who can't get through the day without a tranquilizer; the harried managers who need two or three drinks every night after work to unwind; the young children who try street drugs because they are already touched by our society's bankruptcy of feeling; the college students who go to parties solely to get drunk or stoned; the dangerously fast drivers who are addicted to the thrill of speed; the insider traders who make illegal deals on the stock market because they are addicted to the kick of making money; the perpetual singles who go from lover to lover, addicted to the first glow of romantic love."

Addiction is a negative side of spiritual seeking. To fill this emptiness, we need to reconnect with the capacity for ecstasy that lies dormant within us. We first must understand the nature of ecstasy.

The myth of Dionysus and the rise and fall of this god offer perhaps the best elucidation of the loss of the ecstatic experience.

CHAPTER 30

PROCESS

The Full Life-Cycle Journey from Innovation to Execution

The third layer in *Blueprint* is Process, which explicitly addresses the balance between creativity and execution. This is complementarity in action. Creativity is fluid, open-ended, and inspirational. Once a desired level of creativity is achieved, then execution is required to complete delivery. Execution is buttoned-downed, rigorous, and time-conscious. Creativity and execution are therefore two different modes of consciousness, both essential, and the challenge for process is to find the right balance, and transition, between them.

In particular, as Figure 30-1 suggests, creativity dominates in the early stage of process, yielding over time to an execution mindset for completion. In many cases, the team gets stuck in one or the other mindset, handicapping satisfactory completion. The conscious leader understands the need for both.

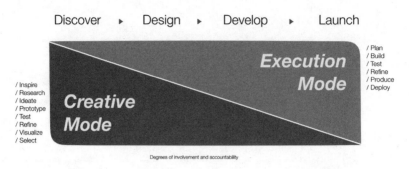

FIGURE 30-1 Two Complementary Modes in Project Evolution

Managing this transition in mindset can be experienced as an unnatural act. It certainly doesn't happen automatically, which may account for the failure of many design operations to produce finished products, and also explain product development projects that deliver products of inferior innovation or quality. The conscious leader understands the need for this transition and the inherent binary aspect of the project development journey and is able to manage the team along that path.

The project development process might then look like the diagram in Figure 30-2.

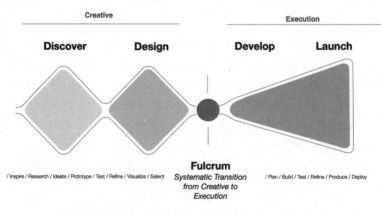

FIGURE 30-2 The Project Development Process

As suggested in the figure, the creative phase may involve several alterations toward the desired outcome. There is an extensive literature on Design Thinking that informs the creative phase, and it is not our purpose to suggest or review those practices here. Also, there are many different forms of process in the execution phase as well. In the latter case, we do believe that the execution phase is best facilitated through the use of strong-form, cross-functional teams where participants representing different functions have specific deliverables over, say, a five-stage process. That approach itself embodies its own internal complementarity with its horizontal, versus vertical, direction of control, and also emphasizes the practice of creative collaboration as a central focus.

The most important aspect of this process is the fulcrum, a systematic transition from the creative phase to the execution phase. The process requires explicit acknowledgment of the need for that transition, which could be memorialized in a specific formal team event.

FEMININE MYTHS

An Inquiry into Imbalance

Recall our discussion of teams as a network, or constellation, of nodes. The constellations were named by our ancestors as a way of understanding and categorizing the random pattern of stars. These names and stories associated with them have nothing to do with nature but may tell us something about ourselves. An interesting question is where did the constellation stories come from? There are 88 constellations in the catalog. Of these, 72 were named animals or things, 12 have masculine names, and 4 have feminine names. Why the imbalance between masculine and feminine?

· · ·

Now look at myths. Again, we find a relative paucity of feminine myths. One clue to this ancient disparity is to look at the *contemporary* version of mythmaking, and there we find an interesting story. In a TED Talk, Christopher Bell talked about his then nine-year-old daughter who is "strong, smart, fast, and fights like a ninja." She loves women superheroes, her favorite being Princess Leia of Star Wars. The problem is that women superheroine costumes and toys are hard to find in stores. There are plenty of princess toys, but very few superheroines. For example, Disney purchased Lucas Films in 2012 and soon flooded the stores with male Star Wars action figures: Luke Skywalker, Obi-Wan Kenobi, Han Solo, and so on. Despite a broad plea to include Leia (#wewantleia) and promises to develop her action toy, over the next three years none appeared. Further, inspired by an iconic scene from the movie where Leia confronts Darth Vader, a T-shirt with that image was created, but with Luke Skywalker replacing Leia.

And that's not all. Marvel's movie *Guardians of the Galaxy* featured Gamora, played by Zoë Saldana. Gamora is a superb fighter with superhuman strength and healing powers. Girls love Gamora, yet in the merchandise associated with the movie, her image is missing from backpacks and T-shirts emblazoned with images of the remaining male figures. Black Widow, a woman superhero in the *Avengers* series, has no action figures in the associated merchandise. In the 30 animated action films planned for the next five years, only 2 include female solo leads.

So, what's going on here? Bell argues that the "public pedagogy," how we learn what we know about other people and about the world, is dominated by six media companies collectively controlling 90% of media production. Evidently, female superheroes mess up the public pedagogy, at least in the eyes of the media companies. But this makes no business sense. Profit-seeking companies are always looking for incremental markets to address. Here's one: millions of young girls wanting superheroine action toys in the midst of a broader culture shaped by decades of the women's movement. It seems a great opportunity for expanded sales and market share.

Perhaps, some deeper factor is at work. What mitigates a more balanced approach in the male–female complementarity? This imbalance brings to mind one of the great unsolved problems in physics, the baryon asymmetry problem—the observed imbalance of matter and anti-matter in the universe. Despite predictions by widely accepted theories of astrophysics that predict symmetry, there isn't much anti-matter to be found. Clearly, the answer to this imbalance resides somewhere in physics, while the masculine-feminine dichotomy exists somewhere in our psyches.

We are seeking lessons for leadership from myths. We have seen a half-dozen male figures, but so far only one female figure: Athena. Half the population deserves more from our mythological tradition.

Inanna

No quest to understand the implications of myth for leadership can ignore the story of the Mesopotamian goddess Inanna, one of the most powerful of ancient myths. Almost 5,000 years ago, Inanna was the "Queen of Heaven" in the Sumerian pantheon and played a more dominant role in myth and hymn than any other deity. We will summarize her myth, suggest some initial interpretations related to leadership and reference sources for interested readers. One main source for the story, and the source of quotations in this summary, is Diane Wolkstein and Samuel Noah Kramer's *Inanna Queen of Heaven: Her Stories and Hymns from Sumer*.

In the beginning were the Great Above, Earth, and the Great Below. Then a single tree, a *huluppu* tree, was planted on the bank of the Euphrates. Inanna took care of the tree for ten years, and eventually Gilgamesh, an earlier demigod, carved a throne and bed for Inanna from the tree. In an act of trickery common to many foundation stories, she met with Enki, God of Wisdom, and basically drank him under the table. Fourteen times Enki drank to Inanna, in total granting her 81 me (attributes of civilization) including "the arts of the hero, the skills of power, the crafts of civilized society, truth, descent into the underworld, ascent from the underworld, the perceptive ear, the rejoicing of the heart, the giving of judgment, and [most importantly] the making of decisions." (Excerpt from theosociety.org.) When he sobered up, Enki tried to recall these divine gifts, but Inanna escaped with them.

The story then shifts to the courtship and marriage of Inanna and Dumuzi, a human shepherd. After her sons grew to manhood, "From the Great Above Inanna opened her ear to the Great Below." (The Sumerian words for *ear* and *wisdom* were identical. "Opening your ear" meant opening your heart and mind to hear wisdom.) Then began the story of The Descent of Inanna, probably the most famous part of the Inanna myth—and the most mysterious. Inanna decides to go to the underworld. The story suggests this was to see her older sister Ereshkigal, Queen of the Great Below and Guardian of the Mysteries of Death, who mourned the death of her husband. Inanna told her faithful servant, Ninshubur, that if she did not return within three days, she should go to the fathers to organize a rescue.

Inanna was required to go through seven gates in the underworld, shedding an article of clothing or piece of jewelry at each gate.

"Naked and bowed low, Inanna entered the throne room."

Ereshkigal approached Inanna. The judges of the underworld passed judgment against her.

"Then Ereshkigal fastened on Inanna the eye of death.
She spoke against her the word of wrath.
She uttered against her the cry of guilt.
She struck her.
Inanna was turned into a corpse,
A piece of rotting meat,
And was hung from a hook on the wall."

When Inanna did not return for three days, Ninshubur went to the fathers to help save her. The first two would not help. The third, Enki, whom Inanna had drunk under the table, was deeply grieved. He took dirt from under his fingernails and created two creatures neither male nor female. They were sent into the underworld like flies to be able to get to its inner core. There they found Ereshkigal in childbirth moaning with pain. The two creatures moaned with her, and showed such compassion that Ereshkigal offered them a gift. They asked for Inanna's corpse, nothing more. Then they sprinkled it with food and the waters of life, and Inanna came back to life.

The judges ruled that Inanna could not return from the underworld without providing a substitute. They suggested her servant Ninshubur, but Inanna refused. They suggested one of her sons, but Inanna refused. Finally, Inanna agreed to substitute her husband Dumuzi, who had not even acknowledged her return from the underworld. Dumuzi would spend six months in the Great Below, alternating with six months on Earth.

• • •

This complex myth has spurred many versions and interpretations down through the ages. Recently, Inanna has been regarded as an important feminine model and that her tale shows the myth as a story of feminine initiation. For our purposes, we can simply note several ways in which the story reflects themes from this book:

- The complementarity between two feminine figures, Inanna and Ereshkigal, suggests two sides to feminine consciousness.
- How empathy saved Inanna when the two figures moved Ereshkigal to forgiveness when she was astonished by their expression of compassion for her suffering in childbirth.
- The power of twinning in these two figures created by Enki.
- Complementarity in Inanna's character between strong solar qualities of action and courage, and the lunar qualities of forgiveness and the search for wisdom.

Perhaps the dramatic shedding of all her jewelry and clothing could be seen as shedding worldly attachments on the way to death and rebirth into her authentic self. Her fierce nature upon her return reflects the emergence of feminine strengths. Contemporary narrative focuses on the need for women to discover their authenticity as part of seizing their true identity. In leadership, this may mean accessing their many powerful feminine qualities instead of simply mimicking masculine qualities.

THE MYTHS THAT MYSTIFY

In a recent TED talk, Devdutt Pattanaik, author and self-taught mythologist, compares the myths of India and the West to demonstrate "how these two fundamentally different sets of beliefs about God, death and heaven help us consistently misunderstand one another." Pattanaik recently held the title of Chief Belief Officer in his company, a not very common position in the Western world. He focused on how cultural factors influence business practices.

. . .

To introduce the role of myth, he tells the story of Ganesha, the elephant-headed god who is the scribe of storytellers, and his brother, the athletic warlord of the gods, Kartikeya.

> The two brothers one day decided to go on a race, three times around the world. Kartikeya leapt on his peacock and flew around the continents and the mountains and the oceans. He went around once, he went around twice, he went around thrice. But his brother, Ganesha, simply walked around his parents once, twice, thrice, and said, "I won." "How come?" said Kartikeya. And Ganesha said, "You went around 'the world.' I went around 'my world.'" What matters more?
>
> If you understand the difference between "the world" and "my world," you understand the difference between logos and mythos. "The world" is objective, logical, universal, factual, scientific. "My world" is subjective. It's emotional. It's personal. It's perceptions, thoughts, feelings, dreams. It is the belief system that we carry. It's the myth that we live in.

He also tells the story of Alexander and the Gymnosophist meeting on the banks of the Indus River. A gymnosophist is known as the "naked philosopher," or a sage who considers worldly things, like clothing, as promoting impurity of the soul. So, they sit around scantly clothed thinking deep thoughts. Alexander asks the Gymnosophist, "What are you doing?" "Nothing," replies the Gymnosophist. "And what are you doing?" he asked Alexander. "Conquering the world." Each thought the other ridiculous.

The discrepancy was rooted in the different cultures underlying their divergent perspectives. Culture, Pattanaik argues, is the particular reaction to nature and the attempt to interpret it in terms of stories, symbols, and rituals. In the Western world, the dominant myth at the time of Alexander (and, arguably, today) was reflected in Homer's *Iliad*. The emphasis was on heroism, honor, and achievement. The belief was that you had only one life to live, and how you live it makes all the difference. Western mythology is filled with heroes: Jason traveling the world; Theseus entering the labyrinth to kill the Minotaur. In India, the dominant myth at the time of Gymnosophist (and arguably today) was reflected in the stories of the Mahabharata. The emphasis also was on heroism, honor, and achievement, but assumed reincarnation, where achievements in a single life are of little or no account. East is infinity, West is one.

In turn, business practices are different. Western practices emphasize process, protocol, and ethics. Indians focus on just getting the job done, bending or breaking the rules if necessary. The result is a familiar sense of dissonance as global forces invoke a collision. One example Pattanaik cites is building a product to invoice hospitals. The actual Eastern process is step A, step B, step C... mostly. How do you routinize "mostly," and how do you write a corresponding software program?

Pattanaik ends with the following: "Understand that you live in the subjective truth, and so does he. Understand it. And when you understand it you will discover something spectacular. You will discover that within infinite myths lies the eternal truth. Who sees it all? Varuna has but a thousand eyes. Indra, a hundred. You and I, only two." The issue here is moral relativism, which we are not professing, but myth does take us to the infinite myths within.

David Brooks, columnist for the *New York Times*, strikes a parallel theme in his piece "In Defense of Big Love." Big loves are the themes that transcend a lifetime: love for country, religious awe, human rights. Small loves concern the daily round of care for family and community, work duties, and health. "A little love is a shepherd protecting his flock."

Brooks' lament is that "in America today some of the little loves are fraying, and big love is almost a foreign language." He quotes Alexis de Tocqueville who wrote "What worries me most [about America] is the danger that, amid all the constant trivial preoccupations of private life, ambition may lose both its force and its greatness, that human passions may grow gentler and at the same time baser, with the result that the progress of the body social may become daily quieter and less aspiring."

Big love is the home of myth, the warehouse of all the great, transcendent themes of life. Myth, too, has become a foreign language, and we go about unaware of the forces constantly working on us. Myth is the dark matter of human behavior, invisible but ubiquitous, independently governing the course of the universe and our personal destinies.

PART V

Blueprint in Action

Implementing Blueprint

CHAPTER 31

BLUEPRINT IN ACTION

An Integrated Framework for High Performance

We have now fully defined *Blueprint*. This framework comprises three layers, four practices, three underlying principles, and the central organizing principle of creative collaboration. This seems like a lot to understand and embrace. However, implementation takes only a few hours of training, with continued follow-up from leadership to ensure full implementation.

We can now describe how these elements fit into a coherent whole, and how this delivers on the promise of driving superior performance.

INTEGRATING COMPONENTS OF THE EXECUTION SYSTEM

Creating a high-performance team without a solid framework is like attempting to cross unfamiliar terrain without a map. Without a plan. Without support. Without a system that enables effective teamwork.

Those who are lucky might make it across, but at what cost? And think how much sooner you—and your team—will get there with a map and a plan. We can now examine the role of each constituent element in the overall system that provides that framework.

The Role of the Three-Layer Model

The three-layer model—Enterprise, Culture, Mindset—exposes the underlying root causes and unacknowledged forces that drive outcome. These three layers are distinct, each involving a different set of factors described in different terminology. Yet together they provide a dynamic, bottom-up model for how team life unfolds. For both the leader and the participant, the model illuminates new territory as a basis for an explicit understanding of execution practice. That is, what was before only dimly understood, or ignored altogether, is now clearly visible. Team members have an expanded and transparent view of the overall operational system.

In particular, introducing the Mindset Layer is a key contribution to understanding the underlying determinative factors for culture. We also see the archetypal nature of the four dimensions of Mindset by identifying mythic figures with each: such as Ares (god of war) with Courage (with Athena as supporting actress), Apollo with Awareness, Aphrodite and Eros with Relatedness, and, of course, Hermes with Agility.

The three-layer model defines *what* we are trying to optimize.

The Role of Principles

Unlike the practices, the three principles—empathy, complementarity, and nonattachment—are more about *attitudes* than activities. They infiltrate all aspects of team operation and inform and facilitate operation of the system. Complementarity, as a basic rule of nature, expands the range of possibility, and enables flexibility and agility. As the "master emotion," empathy is the glue that binds the team. Empathy's biggest contribution is *connectedness*, essential to access the full potential of the team. Nonattachment keeps us out of blind alleys of our own making and facilitates creative flow. These practices reflect psychological health at the individual and team levels. They up our game.

The principles define why *Blueprint* works.

The Role of Practices

From this three-layer model, with its particular dimensions identified, we now have a framework that is *complete*. It is also *actionable* by virtue of the four practices—communication, commitment, closure, and collaboration. We see that, while these practices sound obvious and universal, their effective implementation is more of an art form. There are many ways to communicate, including loud in-your-face confrontation, but communicating in a manner to encourage engagement is a subtler matter. Commitment sounds great, but how many commitments are actually followed by on-time delivery? Our approach includes specific practices that are teachable, easy to understand and repeatable.

The first three—communication, commitment, and closure—have a decisive effect on elevating trust in the team, that bedrock quality without which teams most often fail. The fourth, collaboration, defines the core process supporting creative collaboration by circumventing the common knee-jerk impulse to oppositional dialogue. Our version of collaboration thus provides the gateway to accessing the collective intelligence and creativity of the connected team. The full implementation of the four practices creates a sealed container, diminishing acting out and other forms of internal friction. This container, in turn, provides a self-regulating effect, where problem resolution occurs efficiently at multiple levels as a normal course of business.

The practices define how *Blueprint* works.

The Role of Creative Collaboration as a Central Organizing Principle

The system has creative collaboration as a *central organizing principle* that ties together the various activities associated with driving execution. It also provides engagement and motivation, integrating an individual's aspirations and urges to contribute fully to the operational reality, without attempting to force it.

Engagement and motivation are the desired consequences from *Blueprint*. Recall from Chapter 3 how Gallup determined that over two-thirds of U.S. workers were either "not engaged" or "actively disengaged." Going back to the *Harvard Business Review* classic "Demand Better Results—And Get Them" mentioned in Chapter 12, management guru Robert Schaffer talks about the barriers to achieving high performance and locates the problem with management's failure to set high standards. You can have all the process in the world, and best practices galore, but those alone will not generate results. In a 1991 retrospective, Schaffer says in the *Harvard Business Review*, "The principal reason [for not seeing more progress toward meeting global competitive challenge] is that few managers possess the capacity—or feel compelled—to establish high performance improvement expectations *in ways that elicit results* [italics added]. This capacity continues to be the most universally underdeveloped managerial skill."

Here, we have a clear statement of one of the central unsolved problems in management practice, a "managerial skill" that can "elicit results." The word "elicit" means "to bring or draw out" (i.e., to draw from the well the contribution latent in the team). The reliance of top-down leadership that commands compliance without regard for "eliciting results" constrains organizational performance. Remedying that "most universally underdeveloped managerial skill" has become the new mandate for leadership.

The Role of Myth

One basic hypothesis of this book is that myth informs leadership. The argument is that myth defines our humanity, and leaders are human. Unlike the fish that is last to see the water it swims in, we become aware of how mythological themes permeate our environment and determine our conduct. We believe that bringing these personifications of human nature consciously forward into current time can help inform team behavior. Myths display the full range of human characteristics: honor and dishonor, truth and deceit, courage and cowardice, recklessness and caution, selfishness and selflessness, joy and despair. Myths, with their immense diversity and complexity, are us. With their presence felt in current time, we can consciously choose which of their attributes to model and which to deny.

Let's take a look back at our mythological accounts, one by one, and see more directly how they influence the Execution System.

Narcissus reminds us of serious consequences arising from excessive self-centeredness. We have seen the many corrosive effects of narcissism on team performance. Narcissus also reminds us that being open to other input is an essential step toward avoiding the vegetative state. Narcissism is also the root factor behind idealized fantasies, hubris, inflation, and illusion—all obstacles to establishing the state of "clear mind" for the team. We have learned how to identify narcissism in the workplace, and how the practices provide the means for its confrontation and elimination.

Daedalus and Icarus are a primary example of complementary partnering, but one that failed. Daedalus and Icarus constellate a call to balance between exuberant youth and grounded wisdom, each with its upside and downside attributes. The prevalence of this and other puer/senex stories (e.g., Helios and Phaeton) indicate a common occurrence of puer/senex conflict and suggest a much-needed rebalancing in modern-day team life.

Solar/Lunar Archetypes

My first reaction to my exposure to Howard Teich's solar/lunar complementarity was to experience liberation from the gender wars. We no longer need to have the politically distracting and vexing debate about whether this or that "feminine" or "masculine" quality is superior, and how compliance should be compelled in our cultures.

The solar/lunar categorization provides significant value to the four dimensions of Mindset. These include:

- **For Courage.** Solar Forcefulness, Lunar Fearlessness
- **For Agility.** Solar Flexibility, Lunar Responsiveness
- **For Awareness.** Solar Informed, Lunar Perceptive
- **For Relatedness.** Solar Presence, Lunar Empathy

Solar/Lunar is deeply interlaced throughout *Blueprint*. Perhaps its most important contribution is lunar's association with creativity: the generator of strategy and direction to be handed over to solar to execute. Lunar consciousness is essential to our central theme of creative collaboration. With its themes of intuition, insight, reflection, and even wiliness, lunar has the capacity to unleash a greater level of innovation in the team.

Like puer in puer/senex, Solar seems to be the dominant mode in business, and the lunar aspect may take some getting used to. Elevating the importance of lunar mindset is another case of transitioning from a unitary perspective to one embracing complementarity. The shift to a greater solar/lunar balance may take time, but, like senex, is likely to provide superior results in the long term.

Hercules

Hercules is seen as a hero, renowned for his prodigious strength and spectacular deeds. We took a closer look at him as a model for leadership and found him lacking some essential qualities. He is probably one of the purest solar figures in mythology: unreflective and impetuous. He dramatized for us the shortcomings of the Solo Hero Model of leadership. Like Narcissus, he appears to us more as a warning than a model. His only recourse to lunar qualities is out of desperation when being rescued by Athena.

Athena

Athena, on the other hand, we found to be exquisitely balanced in her solar and lunar qualities. In some sense, the transformation we described in the interlude *From Solo Hero to Complementary Heroes* is very close to the transformation we are promoting for today's leadership. The Solo Hero Model, in trouble, abandons blind adherence to a one-sided approach, and through partnering and a shift to a balanced mindset creates a complementary unit that cures its limitations.

Cultivating Wisdom with Myth

Kwame Scruggs of Alchemy, Inc. not only understood the power of story and myth, he did something with it. His work with the urban youth of Akron, Ohio, rescued many from a likely outcome of poverty and/or crime. The approach seems simple when understood: Connect contemporary youth with the ancient bedrock of myth and the human drama, as a way of illuminating those issues in their current lives. And seek answers. Surely, this experience provides evidence that access to the mythological layer has a powerful effect on shaping our contemporary lives, and soundly refutes the notion that "myth" is just false. Cannot this help leadership as well?

Dionysus and Drama

Noting that drama seemed to be the frequent negative side effect arising from team dysfunction, we explored its mythological basis in the figure of Dionysus. We found, as is usually the case in human experience, that drama has two sides: one the corrosive version we see in poorly led teams, and the other in the legitimate and wholly human search for ecstasy. The alchemical challenge in our organizations is to convert the former into the latter, and we see that while full-blown ecstasy might be a rare experience in the workplace, achieving joy in connection and achievement is well within our grasp.

Inanna

In our search for wisdom from feminine myths—and noting the paucity of girl superheroes in contemporary life—we ran across Inanna as one of the great figures in this category. This ancient Mesopotamian story has received much attention in the search for women's evolution and female roles in today's world. This dramatic tale illustrates the shedding of attachments as a path toward accessing the fierce strength of feminine power. Deepening our understanding of this ancient tale may assist women to move more fully into their rightful role and continue to increase influence that is uniquely theirs.

Maya

Maya also befuddles us by cloaking events in illusion, and Nemesis extracts an exorbitant price for hubris.

Hermes

Hermes is the big guy, a possible contender for the MVP of the Greek pantheon. He is a force of nature, and his richness as a figure possibly arises from his multitudinous complementary aspects. We have seen how his qualities as a connector, trickster, and change agent can play directly into our contemporary team life. He probably embodies more raw material than any other mythological figure and is therefore the most challenging to model. Probably his most attractive qualities for adoption include open communication, creative agility, and the courage to call for organizational enhancements as a change agent.

· · ·

While we started out with the Hero's Journey as a guide to action, we can now see that this book itself represents a journey. The Call was the failure of contemporary leadership, expressed in both survey and results. The Departure was the search for effective methods, often wandering down blind alleys. Helpers along the way showed up in many guises at each stage. And the Return, at least for this cycle, is putting together the account of that journey here.

CHAPTER 32

IMPLEMENTING BLUEPRINT: DEALING WITH RESISTANCE

The Challenge

One final challenge concerns how to fully enable *Blueprint*. Certainly, the path includes adoption of the principles and practices described earlier that lead to enhanced trust, openness, connectedness, collaboration, creativity, and performance. Getting these in place is an important step, but it may not happen all at once and in a predictable sequence. Resistance can come from many quarters. We have seen power plays, intrigue, manipulation, and the impulse to take the system back down to the more familiar state where old habits persist unchallenged, and where the uncomfortable need to move to a higher level of functioning can be eliminated.

In one case, where a turnaround had been achieved, one insightful board member warned the CEO that his success in improving the performance of the organization was in fact an embarrassment to the founders, who would be inclined to return the company to its prior state. Or, even more irrationally, they might simply resent progress, despite the considerable financial gain it provided them, and perhaps even engage in sabotage.

More benign and familiar cases may involve the inertia of those skeptical about any new approach until positive change is evident. We have often said that probably the most important qualification to be a successful entrepreneur is simply persistence. So, just implementing *Blueprint* may need to be augmented by a certain doggedness. In fact, we would call it toughness, a refusal to accept partial results, a rejection of plainly hostile forces, and abandonment where support is not forthcoming. And it is worthwhile to remember that invoking change is like pulling a brick with a rubber band. If you don't pull, it won't move. If you pull too hard, the rubber band will break. Indeed, change is sometimes difficult to see from the inside, and it is a leader's role to point out change as it happens, so as to encourage continued effort.

CHAPTER 33

IMPLEMENTING BLUEPRINT: REALIZING THE BENEFITS

The Reward

For leaders, the benefits of implementing *Blueprint* should be obvious. These show up at the four dimensions of the Enterprise Layer described in Chapter 9, "Dimensions of Culture and Enterprise." Self-regulation and sustainability follow. These lead to *external* success factors such as growth, profitability, and market share. Also, in accordance with the Law of Complementarity, the *internal* factors of increased engagement, well-being, and meaning are realized. At the team member level, the opportunity is to participate in a system that addresses the four key requirements employees seek: to make a contribution, to be recognized for their contribution, to be seen and heard, and to be part of something bigger than themselves. The system also provides the opportunity, as discussed earlier, to "lead from your position" as in the following actions:

- You can better understand your local environment, generate ideas for contribution, and feel free to speak up.
- You can collaborate with your colleagues and offer creative support through empathy/response.
- You can stop toxic gossip when it arrives on your doorstep by identifying the right person for that conversation.
- You can ensure your commitments are authentic and that changes are negotiated in a timely manner.
- You can provide closure in dialogue, see where it isn't happening elsewhere, and suggest remediation.
- You can observe the behavior of the management team and make a more accurate assessment of outcomes.
- You can challenge poor practices when you see them and request remedial attention.
- You can experience the joy of being part of a healthy team and celebrate its achievements.

You can also go further and seek out a business partner, using the twinning method described in Chapter 11. This involves being more than just "buddies," and includes an explicit agreement for unconditional support, full candor, and watching each other's back. As we discussed, this may entail confronting the limiting belief that creating a dependency is a sign of weakness, or that partnering runs the risk of reduced autonomy and control. At that point, you might consider that if the method of the connected team described in this book leads to superior outcomes, then starting with two people surely is a step in the right direction.

We hope you have now gained improved understanding and clarity regarding how teams work—and how you can facilitate that process. We envision two benefits. One is to you, how you can be more effective on your teams, and how you understand and assess your environment. These are personal benefits, preparing you for a better work experience and career. The second benefit is more global—how you can go out and do your part to change the world. Of course, this starts locally, in your immediate work environment, but it then radiates outward—how far it does so none of us knows in advance.

Whether proceeding top down from executives embracing this new mindset or bottom up from team members demonstrating influence from their own position, we all can encourage this type of leadership moving forward. We may find allies from an even broader set of stakeholders and investors as the evidence of superior financial performance mounts. Some will refuse this call, but they risk becoming "a victim to be rescued," if rescued at all. For who but ourselves will take responsibility for refusing to settle for disengagement, lack of creativity, frustrated goals, and failing enterprises?

This journey will also have its challenges and attract naysayers and cynics. What they miss, though, is the exhilaration of immersion in the fray, and the experience of shaping reality versus being ensnared in fantasy. Brené Brown has written about courage and the willingness to lean into a challenge. She reminds us, once we are in the ring committed, we cannot go back. "We now know when we're showing up and when we're hiding out, when we are living our values and when we are not. Our new awareness ... remind(s) us of our commitment to wholeheartedness." Finding the right environment that suits your values may take time and involve false starts. Those are good times to remind ourselves that living with integrity is worth the price.

Welcome to the revolution.

FURTHER READING

Lazlo Back, *Work Rules!: Insights from Inside Google That Will Transform How You Live and Lead*, Hachette, 2015

Scott C. Beardsley, Bradford C. Johnson, and James M. Manyika, "Competitive Advantage Through Better Interactions," *McKinsey Quarterly*, April 2006

John Beebe, *Integrity in Depth*, Texas A&M University Press, 1992 (2005 Reprint edition)

David L. Bradford and Carole S. Robin, *Leadership Excellence and the "Soft" Skills: Authenticity, Influence and Performance*, Stanford Graduate School of Business, 2004

Nathan Robert Brown and Evans Lansing Smith, Ph.D., *The Complete Idiot's Guide to World Mythology*, Alpha, 2008

Betsy Burroughs, https://www.focuscatalyst.com

Joseph Campbell, *The Hero with a Thousand Faces*, Princeton University Press, 1968

Mihaly Csikszentmihalyi, *Finding Flow: The Psychology of Engagement with Everyday Life* (1998) and *Flow: The Psychology of Optimal Experience* (2008)

Amy Edmondson, "Psychological Safety and Learning Behavior in Work Teams," *Administrative Science Quarterly*, June 1999

Clarissa Pinkola Estés, *Women Who Run with the Wolves: Myths and Stories of the Wild Woman Archetype*, Ballantine Books, 1996

Benjamin Franklin, *The Autobiography of Benjamin Franklin*, Dover Reprint Edition, 2016

John Gerzema and Michael D'Antonio, *The Athena Doctrine: How Women (and the Men Who Think Like Them) Will Rule the Future*, Jossey-Bass, 2013

Daniel Goleman, *Emotional Intelligence: Why It Can Matter More Than IQ*, Bantam, 1995

Daniel Goleman and Richard E. Boyatzis, "Social Intelligence and the Biology of Leadership," *Harvard Business Review*, September 2008

James Hillman, *Senex and Puer: Uniform Edition of the Writings of James Hillman*, Vol. 3 (James Hillman Uniform Edition), Spring Publications, 2005

Robert A. Johnson, *Ecstasy: Understanding the Psychology of Joy*, Harper, 1989

C.G. Jung (Commentary by), *The Secret of the Golden Flower: A Chinese Book of Life*, Richard Wilhelm (Translator), Cary F. Baynes (Translator), reprint of 1931 edition, Martino Fine Books, 2014

C.G. Jung, *Memories, Dreams, and Reflections*, Reprint edition, Vintage, 1989

Rich Karlgaard and Michael S. Malone, *Team Genius: The New Science of High-Performing Organizations*, Harper Business, 2015

Marina Krakovsky, "Lean Startup and Design Thinking: Getting the Best Out of Both," *Stanford Graduate School of Business*, 2016

Charles Krauthammer, *Things That Matter: Three Decades of Passions, Pastimes and Politics*, Crown Forum, 2013

Rick Levine, et al., *The Cluetrain Manifesto: The End of Business as Usual*, Basic Books, 2001

General Stanley McChrystal, https://www.mcchrystalgroup.com/insights/

David McCollough, *The American Spirit: Who We Are and What We Stand For*, Simon & Schuster, 2017

Michel de Montaigne, http://media.bloomsbury.com/rep/files/primary-source-77-michel-de-montaigne-on-the-education-of-children.pdf

William Ouchi, *The M-Form Society: How American Teamwork Can Recapture the Competitive Edge*, Addison-Wesley, 1984

M. Scott Peck, *In Search of Stones: A Pilgrimage of Faith, Reason, and Discovery*, Hyperion, 1995

Daniel F. Prosser, *Thirteeners: Why Only 13 Percent of Companies Successfully Execute Their Strategy—and How Yours Can Be One of Them*, Geenleaf Book Group Press, 2015

Julia Rozovsky, "The Five Keys to a Successful Google Team," https://rework.withgoogle.com/blog/five-keys-to-a-successful-google-team, 2015

Robert H. Schaffer, "Demand Better Results—And Get Them," *Harvard Business Review*, March–April 1991

Joshua Wolf Shenk, "The Power of Two," *Atlantic Magazine*, July 2014

Howard Teich, Ph.D., *Solar Light, Lunar Light: Perspectives in Human Consciousness*, Genoa House, 2012

Paul J. Zak, "The Neuroscience of Trust," *Harvard Business Review*, January–February 2017

ACKNOWLEDGMENTS

I have been having an open and creative collaboration about the future of leadership with an amazing network of friends and colleagues. In many ways this vigorous dialogue prefigured this book, in turn a textual record of what preceded it. Their frequent insistence to "Hurry up. We badly need this" was an important encouragement to me to continue the slog that any book requires to reach completion. I wanted to express my appreciation to each.

Dr. Howard Teich made principal contributions to this book, including our collaboration on the centrality of complementarity, his work on the problem of idealized expectations (and inventing the term "Cancer of the Mind"), the development of the diagnostic three-layer model, his groundbreaking work discovering the solar/lunar archetypes, and his focus on the importance and implementation of empathy. He has been one of those wonderful, lifetime partners encouraging this project at every step. Claudia Riemer Boutote, of Red Raven Studio, is an amazing agent and editor and an uncommonly creative partner in collaboration. Her support made all the difference. My long-term friend and partner Dr. Dan Thomas provided enormous support throughout this project including, but not limited to, suggesting the title Real Teams Win. Linda Hayes, also a long-term partner, hung in there through uncountable drafts to patiently offer suggestions, make introductions to her considerable network, and sustain encouragement. Blaise Bertrand, who showed up in the last few years as another cherished future long-term partner, also motivated completion of the book, along with contributing his amazing graphic support. Terry Pearce (in memoriam) was a career-long mentor and partner, and a model for articulating a more human-centric leadership through his multiple publications. Jan Hunter, exceptionally gifted editor who taught me how writing proceeds "bit by bit" and patiently worked with this probably most challenging of clients. Tuck Newport, friend and former Stanford Sloan Program classmate, exhibited an astonishing generosity through painstakingly reviewing an early draft. He taught me a great deal about clear writing and encouraged staying the course to relevance. Thomas Moore, someone whose work on soul I followed and voraciously consumed, also generously reviewed an early draft and encouraged completion. Professor Dennis Slattery likewise generously provided a most helpful review and made several key suggestions for its improvement. His immense, worldwide reputation as a leading mythologist added heft and emphasis to understanding the importance of the "mythic layer" in the book. Betsy Burroughs, good friend and genius-level marketing executive, made critical contributions and offered helpful introductions to other interested parties. My great, long-term friend John Steinhart generously provided what he has always done over our 40-year friendship: valuable input and ongoing encouragement. Martha Sintz who also got behind the importance of the topic and allocated hours to review and commentary. Anna Mehrotra whose sharp insight helped immeasurably making the text more readable and relevant. Ria Mehrotra, gifted budding artist, for her thoughts on the book cover. Other family members, Doug, Ateev, and LeeAnn for their patient support over a long and sustained project. Richard Adler, Distinguished Fellow at the Institute for the Future, generously listened to the presentation on *Blueprint* and make the critical connection to Stanley McChrystal's similar work in *Team of Teams*. Nick Copping for his ongoing support as well as hosting a workshop on the material in the book. Doug Cole for his patient reading of drafts and continuing encouragement and support. Steve Aizenstat, Chancellor, and Joseph Cambray, CEO of Pacifica Graduate Institute for their encouragement, introductions to some amazing faculty, and supporting my presence on their board of trustees. Dr. Neora Myrow for her brilliant conversational ability and her willingness to share her extraordinary knowledge over multiple long conversations. Dr. Kwame Scruggs for his amazing work in helping urban youth through his Alchemy Inc. initiative. Dr. Maren Hansen for her comments on Inanna based on a vastly superior knowledge on that important myth. David Lane and Skip Vaccarello (author *Finding God in Silicon Valley*) for their encouragement and in anticipation of future collaboration). Reid Rutherford for his contribution to our joint workshop. Nancy Chou, Kip Quackenbush and Tony Price for their support and enthusiasm about *Blueprint*. Finally, for my wife Carole's support, the central figure behind the scenes that accepted as an article of faith the necessity of my writing this book, and graciously put up with many hours of distraction.

INDEX

3Com, 162–163
24-Hour Rule, 195

achievement, 216
Adams, John, 148
addiction, 217
Adler, Richard, 22
admitting wrong, 115
agility, 51, 137
alchemy, 205
Alchemy, Inc., 183–186, 241
Alcoholics Anonymous, 80
Alexander and the Gymnosophist, 230
Amdahl, Carl, 17
America: Imagine a World Without Her (D'Souza), 129
The American Spirit (McCullough), 148
anticipated empathy, 130
Aphrodite, 8
Apollo, 71–72
Apple, 80
The Archetypal Imagination (Fay), 17–18
archetypes
    puer/senex, 103–105
    solar/lunar, 91–93, 239–240
    Wise Old Man, 105
Ares, 8, 96–98
Aston Martin Lagonda Ltd., 133
Athena, 9, 96–99, 240–241
The Athena Doctrine (Gerzema and D'Antonio), 97, 98
Atlas, 71
Autobiography (Franklin), 113–115
awareness, 51

Bacchus, 215
bad advice. *See* false teachings
Barrett, Craig, 80
Beatles, the, 101
Beebe, John, 119–120
Bell, Christopher, 223
Bendor, Jonathan, 165
Benhamou, Eric, 163
big loves, 231
Blanchard, Ken, 171–172
Blueprint framework
    dealing with resistance, 243–244
    diagnostic model, 33
    integrating components of the execution system, 235–242
    overview, 2
    practices of, 33
    principles of, 31–32
    process, 33
    realizing the benefits, 245–247
    surrendering the ego, 6–7
    system architecture, 31–33
Bock, Laszlo, 21
Book III of *Metamorphoses* (Ovid), 143
bottom-up planning, vs. top-down planning, 89
Boy Who Cried Wolf myth, 37
Bradford, David, 101
Bridge Communications, 162
Bridgewater Associates, 120–121
Brin, Sergey, 80
Brooks, David, 231
Brown, Brené, 247
Built on Trust (Steding and Ciancutti), 23, 62
Burroughs, Betsy, 27–28
business failures, categories of, 18

California Department of
    Transportation, 63
Call, the, 38
    See also Hero's Journey
Calypso, 73
Cambray, Joseph, 26
Campbell, Joseph, 35, 37–39, 183
    See also Hero's Journey
"Capital M marketing," 130–131
    See also marketing
capitalism, 129–130
Challenger space shuttle, 179, 181
Churchill, Winston, 150
Circe, 73
Cisco, 163
clarity, 199
closure, 193
    developing a culture of, 195–197
    recognizing the consequences of
        non-closure, 194–195
    tracking, 197–199
coherence, 63–64
collaboration, 63, 137
    and consensus, 127
    how to do empathy, 123–127
    See also creative collaboration
Columbia Accident Investigation
    Board (CAIB), 180
Columbia space shuttle, 179–181
commitment, 187–188
    authentic, 191–192
    false commitments lead to drama,
        188–189
    quality of, 189–190
    renegotiating as necessary, 190
    taking the time to consider, 189
communication
    catastrophic consequences of poor
        communication, 179–182
    constant, 175–177
    direct, 173
    inclusive, 171–173
    indirect, 176–177
    open, 171
    overview, 169–171
    resolving conflict quickly, 176

respectful, 175–176
truthful, 173–175
competition, vs. cooperation, 87
*Competitive Advantage Through Better
    Interactions*, 19–21
complementarity, 31, 32, 201, 236
    defined, 77
    examples in nature, 77–78
    mythological basis of, 71–75
    as a solution to paradoxical
        physical phenomena, 78–79
    twinning, 79–81
    two axes of, 85–90
    See also twinning
*The Complete Idiot's Guide to World
    Mythology* (Smith), 37
conflict, 176
conflict of the opposites, 92–93
consensus, collaboration and, 127
content, vs. process focus, 88
contribution, 216
cooperation, vs. competition, 87
courage, 50, 55
Covey, Stephen M.R., 63
creative capacity, 29–30
creative collaboration, 19–24,
    210–211
    and the network model of
        leadership, 26
    the role of, 237–238
    See also collaboration
creative consciousness, in the team,
    131–134
Creative Destruction, 153–154
Creative Mode, 85–86
creativity, 82, 219–221
Crick, Francis, 78
Cronus, 104
Csikszentmihalyi, Mihaly, 150
cultural fabric, 201, *202*
customer intimacy, 64
cynicism, 192

Daedalus and Icarus, 107–109, 239
D'Antonio, Michael, 97
dark energy, 211

dark matter, 211
deep imagination, 26
Demand Results--And Get Them
(Schaffer), 86
denial, 192
Departure, the, 39–40
See also Hero's Journey
dependability, 198
depth perspective, 2
Design Thinking, 136–137, 221
despair, 39–40
Development Dimensions
International, 133
DiMaggio, Dennis, 133
Dionysus, 213–217, 241
Dirac, Paul, 78
directed passion, 104
DNA, 78
drama, 188–189
and Dionysus, 213–217, 241
DreamWorks, 154–155
D'Souza, Dinesh, 129–130

EBITDA, 19–20
Echo, 143
Ecstasy (Johnson), 216
Edmondson, Amy, 21
ego, surrendering, 6–7
Einstein, Albert, 78
electricity and magnetism, 78
Emerging Global Structure, 26
emotion, 32
emotional integrity, 119–121
emotional intelligence (EI), 112–113,
117
Emotional Intelligence (Goleman),
112–113
empathy, 31, 32, 201, 236
evolving an empathic mindset,
113–115
gauging and improving, 115–117
in leadership, 112–113
marketing and, 129–137
in the message architecture,
134–136
neuroscience of, 111–112

empathy/challenge, 123–127
employees, what employees want,
69–70
Empowered Execution, 23
execution, 82, 219–221
Execution Mode, 86
external success factors, 245

"fail fast" concept, 154
failure
categories of business failures, 18
paradox of success and failure,
153–155
of startups, 16–18
fake teams, vs. real teams, 5–6
false teachings, 40
Fat Startup, 137
Fay, Carolyn, 17–18
Fay, Ernest, 17–18
The Federalist Papers, 45
feeling, 53–54
feminine myths, 223–227
feminine/masculine traits, 97–98
Feynman, Richard, 215
flow, 150
Ford, 133
Frankenberg, Bob, 161–162
Franklin, Benjamin, 113–115

Gaia, 104
gambler mindset, 17
Ganesha, 229–231
The Gathering Storm (Churchill), 150
Geffen, David, 154
Gehman, Hal, 180
Gerzema, John, 97
Golden State Warriors, 170
Goleman, Daniel, 81, 112–113
gossip, 176–177
Grove, Andy, 80

The Heart Aroused (Whyte), 88–89
Helpers Along the Way, 40–41
See also Hero's Journey
Hera, 71, 95, 143, 214
Hercules, 8, 9, 95–98, 240

Hermes, 9, 71–75, 242
Hermetic method, 9
The Hero with a Thousand Faces
    (Campbell), 37, 39
Hero's Journey
    the Call, 38
    the Departure, 39–40
    despair, 39–40
    false teachings, 40
    Helpers Along the Way, 40–41
    impatience, 39
    myths and, 35
    the Return, 41
Hewlett, Bill, 80
Hewlett-Packard, 83
hierarchical leadership model, 13–18
Hillman, James, 105, 192
The Hobbit, 37
hubris, 162–163

idealized expectations, 157–159
    willing blindfulness, 160–165
idealized fantasies, 157, 160–165
Iguodala, Andre, 170
Iliad (Homer), 72–73
illusion, 163–165
imaginative mind, vs. rational mind,
    28
imbalance between masculine and
    feminine, 223–227
impatience, 39
implementation, 64
improvisation, 126
In Search of Stones (Peck), 57
Inanna, 224–227, 241–242
Inanna Queen of Heaven (Wolkstein
    and Kramer), 225
inferior function, 54
inflation, 160–162
innovation, 64
*An Inquiry into the Nature and
    Causes of the Wealth of Nations*
    (Smith), 129
integrity, 215
interactions, 26
    See also network leadership model

internal success factors, 245
intuition, 53–54

Jackson, Michael, 104
James, LeBron, 170
Jobs, Steve, 80, 96
Johnson, Robert, 216
Johnston, Theresa, 165
Jones, Jim, 96
Jonestown mass suicide, 96
Jung, Carl, 3, 29–30, 53, 132

Karlgaard, Rich, 80, 96
Kartikeya, 229–231
Katzenberg, Jeffrey, 154–155
Keats, John, 139–140
Kerr, Steve, 170
Kramer, Samuel Noah, 225
Krauthammer, Charles, 153

Langewiesche, William, 180
Law of Complementarity, 79, 245
    See also complementarity
leadership
    hierarchical leadership model,
        13–18
    and myth, 7–10
    network leadership model, 25–30
*Leadership Excellence and the "Soft"
    Skills* (Bradford and Robin),
    101
leakage, 203–205
Lean Startup, 136–137
Lennon, John, 101
The Lion King, 37
Livingston, Shaun, 170
Lublin, Joann S., 132–133
Lucas, George, 26, 37

Madison, James, 45
Maia, 71
Malone, Michael, 80, 96
management, "gardener" style of, 23
marketing, and empathy, 129–137
Markman, Art, 141
matter and anti-matter, 78

Maxwell, James Clerk, 78
Maya, 164, 242
McCartney, Paul, 101
McChrystal, Stanley, 22–24
McCullough, David, 148
McLean, Margot, 105
meaning, 83
merging, 80
message architecture, 133–136
Metamorphoses (Ovid), 109
Michelangelo, 28
Microsoft, 161
Miescher, Friedrich, 78
Milky Way Brain, 27–28
mindset, 48–52
Mindset malware
    examples, *58*
    overcoming, 58–59
    trends in Mindset dimensions,
        59–60
mindset malware, 57
minimum viable product (MVP),
    41, 136
mirroring, 80
Montaigne, Michel Eyquem de, 115
Moore, Gordon, 80
Moyer, Bill, 37
Murphy, Kate, 141
Musk, Elon, 26
myth, 37–38
    cultivating wisdom with, 183–186,
        241
    feminine myths, 223–227
    and the hero's journey, 35
    and leadership, 7–10
    mythological basis of
        complementarity, 71–75
    myths that mystify, 229–231
    the role of, 238–242
    Solo Hero myth, 95–96
    See also specific myths

narcissism, 6–7, 9, 147–151
    eliminating via nonattachment,
        150–151
Narcissistic Personality Disorder, 149

Narcissus, 9, 143–145
    lessons from, 147–151
NASA, 179–182
negative capability, 139–140
network leadership model, 25–30
The Neuroscience of Trust (Zak), 63
New York Times, 141
Nike, 97
nonattachment, 31, 32, 137, 139–141,
    201, 236–237
    eliminating narcissism via,
        150–151
    and idealized expectations,
        158–159
Novell, 160–161
Noyce, Robert, 80

Obama, Michelle, 186
objectives, vs. strategy, 87–88
Odysseus, 73
Odyssey (Homer), 73
The One-Minute Manager
    (Blanchard), 171–172
one-on-one meetings, vs. team, 88
organizational habit, 197
organization-as-machine metaphor,
    13–14
Osheroff, Douglas, 181
Ouchi, William, 211

Packard, David, 80
Page, Larry, 80
Pan, 9–10
paradox of success and failure,
    153–155
partnering, 80
    See also twinning
Pattanaik, Devdutt, 229–231
Peck, Scott, 57
peer relationships, 89
People's Temple, 96
performance, 82
persistent business problems,
    psychological root of, 3
Peter Pan Syndrome, 104
Phaeton and Helios, 109

Poseidon, 107–108
The Power of Myth, 37
Powers of Two (Shenk), 101
practices
    the role of, 237
    See also closure; collaboration;
        commitment; communication
Prager, Daniel, 192
Priam, 72–73
principles
    the role of, 236–237
    written statement of operation
        principles, 177
    See also specific principles
process focus, vs. content, 88
project development process,
    220–221
Prosser, Daniel, 191
Proteus, 24
psychological safety, 21–22, 198
public pedagogy, 224
puer, 104
puer/senex archetypes, 103–105
    mythic basis for, 107–109

radiation effect, 208–211
radical transparency, 120
The Rational Bible (Prager), 192
rational mind, vs. imaginative mind,
    28
real teams, vs. fake teams, 5–6
recognition, 216
relatedness, 51, 59–60, 137
resistance
    dealing with, 243–244
    to twinning, 81–83
Return, the, 41
    See also Hero's Journey
revenge, 192
Rhea, 104, 214
Robin, Carole, 101
Rojcewicz, Peter M., 126
Rozovsky, Julia, 21

safety, psychological, 21–22
safety in principles, 177

Saturn, 104–105
Schaffer, Robert, 86, 238
Schoenfeld, Bruce, 170
Schumpeter, Joseph, 153–154
SCI, 158–159
Science Applications International
    Corporation (SAIC), 159
Scruggs, Kwame, 35, 183–186, 241
sealed container, 204–205
Searls, David "Doc," 32
The Secret of the Golden Flower (Jung),
    29–30
self-betrayal, 192
self-centeredness, 147–151
self-regulating organization, 207–211
senex, 104–105
*Senex and Puer: Uniform Edition of
    the Writings of James Hillman*
    (McLean), 105
sensation, 53–54
shared consciousness, 23
Shaw, George Bernard, 175
Shenk, Joshua Wolf, 101
silent majority, 15–16
slipstreaming, 150
Smith, Adam, 129–130
Smith, Bob, 80
Smith, Lans, 37
*Social Intelligence and the Biology of
    Leadership* (Goleman), 81
soft practice, 20
    See also creative collaboration
solar addiction, 82, 92
Solar Light Lunar Light (Teich), 92
solar thinking, 91
solar/lunar balance, 91–93
solar/lunar complementarity, 98
Solo Hero myth, 9, 17, 82, 95–96,
    241
    contemporary refutation of, 101
speed, 64
The SPEED of TRUST (Covey), 63
Spielberg, Steven, 154
staff meetings, 89
Stanford Magazine, 181
Star Wars, 37

startup failure, 16–18
strategic vs. tactical, 89–90
strategy, vs. objectives, 87–88
structure, 199
success, 153–155
    external and internal success
        factors, 245
superheroes, female, 223–224
superior function, 54
sustainable advantage, 65

tacit activities, 19, 20
    See also creative collaboration
Team Genius (Karlgaard and
        Malone), 80, 96
Team of Teams (McChrystal), 22–24
teams, vs. one-on-one meetings, 88
tech support rage, 141
Teich, Howard, 91, 92, 125–126,
        239
A Theory of Moral Sentiments (Smith),
        129
Things That Matter (Krauthammer),
        153
thinking, 53–54
Thirteeners (Prosser), 191
Thomas, Dan, 158
three-layer model
    bottom-up progression, 48–50
    Culture layer, 47–48, 61–64
    Enterprise layer, 46, 64–65
    Mindset layer, 48–53, 236

overview, 45–46
    the role of, 236
Tocqueville, Alexis de, 231
top-down planning, vs. bottom-up
        planning, 89
transcendence, 216
transparency, 64, 120
trickster archetype, 71–75
trust, 62–63
Twain, Mark, 197
Twelve Labors of Hercules, 95, 97
twinning, 22
    complementarity, 79–81
    defined, 79
    resistance and benefits, 81–83

Uranus, 104
U'Ren, Nick, 170

Wall Street Journal, 132–133
The Water of Life, 184
Watson, James, 78
wave-particle duality, 77–78
Whyte, David, 88–89
Wilson, Bill, 80
Wise Old Man archetype, 105
The Wizard of Oz, 37
Wolkstein, Diane, 225
women superheroes, 223–224

Zak, Paul, 63
Zeus, 71, 95, 98, 104, 109, 214

ABOUT THE AUTHOR

Thomas L. Steding, Ph.D. has been pursuing his interest in building high performance teams his entire career. He has been CEO of 13 startup companies and chairman and advisor to many others. He was co-author of *Built on Trust: Gaining Competitive Advantage in Any Organization* (McGraw Hill 2000). His role as a member of the Board of Trustees of Pacifica Graduate Institute reflects his parallel interest in archetypal psychology and its application to leadership and culture.

More Titles From Humanix Books You May Be Interested In:

BEN STEIN
New York Times Bestselling Author
THE
CAPITALIST
CODE
It Can Save Your Life
AND MAKE YOU VERY RICH!

Warren Buffett says:
"My friend, Ben Stein, has written a short book that tells you everything you need to know about investing (and in words you can understand). Follow Ben's advice and you will do far better than almost all investors (and I include pension funds, universities and the super-rich) who pay high fees to advisors."

In his entertaining and informative style that has captivated generations, beloved *New York Times* bestselling author, actor, and financial expert Ben Stein sets the record straight about capitalism in the United States — it is not the "rigged system" young people are led to believe.

Scott Carpenter, Astronaut, NASA's Mercury Project says:
"By following the advice in The Simple Heart Cure, you can surmount the biggest challenge of all and win your battle against heart disease."

Heart disease kills more people than any other medical condition. In *The Simple Heart Cure*, you'll find this top doc's groundbreaking approach to preventing and reversing heart disease — an approach honed by his study of foreign cultures free of heart disease and decades of experience helping patients achieve a healthier heart at any age.

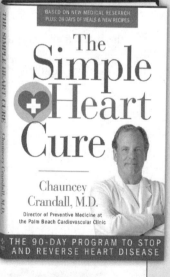

BASED ON NEW MEDICAL RESEARCH
PLUS: 28 DAYS OF MEALS & NEW RECIPES

The
Simple
+ Heart
Cure

Chauncey
Crandall, M.D.

Director of Preventive Medicine at
the Palm Beach Cardiovascular Clinic

THE 90-DAY PROGRAM TO STOP
AND REVERSE HEART DISEASE

For additional information on these and other titles published by Humanix Books, visit:

www.HumanixBooks.com/Free